P9-CDA-373

BOOTH TARKINGTON
1869-1946

MY AMIABLE UNCLE

Recollections about Booth Tarkington

by
Susanah Mayberry

with an Introduction by
James Woodress

PURDUE UNIVERSITY PRESS
West Lafayette, Indiana

Second printing, May 1984

Photograph of Erwin Panofsky courtesy of
Gerda Panofsky. Other photographs
courtesy of the author and her family.

Since Booth Tarkington's portrait collection
was sold to individuals unknown to us, we
were unable to obtain permission to use a
photographic reproduction of Dobson's
John Milton and Lely's Nell Gwyn. We hope
the current owners of the portraits agree
that we have made good use of the works.

Book design by James McCammack

Published 1983

Library of Congress Catalog Card
Number 82-81021

International Standard Book Number
0-911198-66-0 05-24-05

Printed in the United States of America

For Frank

CONTENTS

PREFACE

WHY WOULD ANYONE WANT TO WRITE ABOUT BOOTH Tarkington? Further, why would anyone want to read a book about him?

For several years I have been trying to answer the first question. I gave the obvious reasons, and I really believed them. I said I wanted to share my knowledge of Uncle Booth with family members who did not know him, as well as with future generations, and thus achieve family continuity. That sounded nice when said aloud, and it was really true. But to myself I thought "approval," "pride in having a book published," and, yes, "pride in being able to write a book." However, I continued to feel that I was secretly pursuing my own ends, even though I had no idea what they were. Some element of my real motive still eluded me. I knew, though, that there was more than either family continuity or personal pride involved, but what was it?

It was my husband who finally answered that question for me. I wrote this book, he said, because I wanted to relive my happy times with Uncle Booth. I am his great-niece and knew him for twenty-five years. I cannot think of a greater privilege. The miracle is that during that time I was conscious of how very happy I was. My life now gallops by faster and faster and I forget many things, but happiness such as I experienced with Uncle Booth has its own adhesive quality. To put it simply, happiness sticks. Those very nearly perfect days with Uncle Booth are still vivid memories. Although I realize I can never really relive them, there is a way to recapture their essence. I can — and did — write them down.

As for my second question: why would anyone want to read about Booth Tarkington? You will know why as you read these recollections. He was a greater man than writer. No one who knew Booth

Tarkington ever forgot him. I will spare you a list of superlatives. His qualities will become evident to you as you read, just as they were evident to his loving family and devoted friends. For twenty-five years Fortune smiled upon me. She does so again as I recreate and share long-gone happiness with you.

ACKNOWLEDGMENTS

I OWE A GREAT DEBT TO THE PEOPLE WHO HAVE AIDED ME in the completion of this book. My gratitude goes to Laura Bamberger whose unflagging love during her life meant more to me than I can say. I thank Joe Galimi for his unstinting support to me and encouragement for the book. I am indebted to James Woodress for his gracious permission to use his biography *Booth Tarkington: Gentleman from Indiana* as a major source and to Gerda Panofsky for her kind permission to use excerpts from letters written to my uncle by her husband, Erwin Panofsky. Margaret Dean; the late Margaret Jameson; Richard Ludwig; Hans A. A. Panofsky; Elinor Schmidt; and Percy Simmons; as well as the *Indianapolis Star* and the *Indianapolis News* — all contributed critiques, background information, or specialized knowledge for this work; and I thank them.

I have made two valued friends during the publication of the book. Verna Emery of the Purdue University Press has given her enthusiasm and her editorial skills. She introduced me to Paul Fatout, a professor emeritus of English from Purdue and distinguished Twain scholar. He had an unerring eye for detail, and his appraisal and criticism of this work were invaluable. In addition, he became another good friend — one who is greatly missed.

I owe my deepest thanks to my husband and best friend for his interest, patience, and succor. He knew my manuscript could become a book long before I did.

I am grateful to the following for permission to quote from copyrighted works:

Excerpt from *Booth Tarkington: A Biographical and Bibliographical Sketch* by Asa Don Dickinson. Copyright 1926 by Doubleday and Company, Inc. Used by permission of Doubleday and Company, Inc.

To the *Saturday Evening Post* for quotes and condensed material from "As I Seem to Me" by Booth Tarkington. Copyright 1941 by the Curtis Publishing Company.

Excerpts from *Penrod,* copyright 1913, 1914 by Booth Tarkington. Reprinted by permission of Doubleday and Company, Inc.

Excerpts from *Some Old Portraits* by Booth Tarkington. Copyright 1939 by Booth Tarkington. Published 1939 by Doubleday and Company, Inc. Used by permission of Brandt and Brandt.

To James Woodress for quotations from *Booth Tarkington: Gentleman from Indiana.* Copyright with author. Published 1955. Reprinted 1968 by Greenwood Press, Westport, Connecticut.

To Houghton Mifflin Company for permission to quote from *The Collector's Whatnot* by Booth Tarkington, Kenneth L. Roberts, and Hugh M. Kahler.

To House of Books for permission to quote from *Lady Hamilton and Her Nelson* by Booth Tarkington.

To the Princeton University Library for quotations from *Dr. Panofsky and Mr. Tarkington: An Exchange of Letters, 1938–1946,* edited by Richard M. Ludwig; *On Plays, Playwrights, and Playgoers: Selections from the Letters of Booth Tarkington to George C. Tyler and John Peter Toohey, 1918–1925,* edited by Alan S. Downer; and "The Tarkington Papers," edited by Alexander Wainwright, in the *Princeton University Library Chronicle.*

INTRODUCTION

by James Woodress

WHEN I JOINED THE FACULTY OF BUTLER UNIVERSITY IN the fall of 1950, I was interested in seeing the city that Booth Tarkington had made famous. His novels and stories had delighted me when I was a high school student in Missouri, and I began to reread his works. I soon discovered that despite the great changes that had overtaken central Indiana following World War II Tarkington's fiction still was a good introduction to the social and cultural milieu of Indianapolis. As my interest in Tarkington grew, I decided to direct my scholarly efforts into a study of his life and work, and I was able to find a cousin who could introduce me to Susanah Tarkington, the author's widow. As it happened, she lived only a few blocks from where I had bought a house in Indianapolis. I met Mrs. Tarkington and immediately was attracted to her. She was a great lady, a *grande dame* of the sort I think is now extinct, and knowing her was one of the great experiences of my life. The memory of her casts a nostalgic glow over my early years in Indianapolis. She opened the vast Tarkington archives at Princeton University to me, and I embarked on a biography of her husband. He had been dead only since 1946, and the contents of his study, which had been hauled off to Princeton in a moving van after his death, had not yet been used by scholars. It was an inexhaustible source of material for a biographer, and I happily plunged into writing Tarkington's life.

Meantime, I was teaching at Butler, and one fall early in my years there, Tarkington's niece Susanah Mayberry enrolled in one of my classes. She had been out of Smith for a number of years but was

---

This introduction is a slightly revised version of an address given before the Indiana Historical Society in Indianapolis on March 30, 1979. It is reprinted here with the kind permission of the society.

1

then interested in getting a master's degree and teaching, both of which she did. This relationship also developed into a friendship that has lasted some thirty years. It is a pleasure to supply an introduction for Susanah Mayberry's memoirs of her uncle Booth. Her memories bring her "amiable uncle" to life and complement nicely my outsider's biography. Readers of Tarkington's novels and stories and students of American literature and culture will be glad to have her account available, for Tarkington is a writer of significance who deserves to be read more today than he is. I hope that Susanah Mayberry's book will send people back to the fiction of Booth Tarkington.

Besides the pleasures of reading the work of a witty, born storyteller, the large shelf of novels and stories that Tarkington wrote between 1900 and 1946 provide important insights into the urban development and the social mobility of the American Midwest during the years it was changing from an agrarian postfrontier society to the industrial heartland of the United States. Just as the novels of Faulkner's Mississippi or Willa Cather's Nebraska encapsulate in their art the social, political, and cultural history of their regions, so does Tarkington's work serve as a paradigm of growth in the Midwest. What happens in Tarkington's fiction is representative of what was happening in Saint Louis, Columbus, Cincinnati, or Kansas City.

Tarkington's work belongs in the mainstream of the realistic novel that developed in the United States in the years following the Civil War. The great writers of the late nineteenth century, Howells, James, and Twain, all belong to this tradition; and Tarkington, as one of the next generation of writers, carried on in the manner of these predecessors. The socio-economic novels of Howells, the international novels of James, the boy stories of Twain — all find their exemplars in Tarkington's *oeuvre.* Howells in particular was Tarkington's role model, and I would like to focus on this relationship beginning with the year 1885.

At that time Howells was the leading American novelist. The most discriminating readers, including Howells himself, recognized the importance of Henry James, but most people thought Howells more important. Mark Twain, on the other hand had far more readers than either Howells or James, but people did not equate humor with art. In November 1884 the *Century Magazine* began serializing Howells's novel *The Rise of Silas Lapham.* A fourteen-year-old boy in Indianapolis named Booth Tarkington was reading that serial and could hardly wait from one monthly installment to the next. When the March 1885 issue came with the chapter describing a particularly dramatic episode, the Corey's dinner party for the *nouveau riche* Laphams, young Booth was waiting for the postman. He wanted to be the first in the family to find out what happened to

Silas at the famous dinner. Many years later Tarkington remembered the scene vividly. He wrote in an article on the occasion of Howells's death in 1920 that "I had seized upon the parcel, opened it, and, like a pig indeed, had read the precious installment in a hidden retreat." As he finished and came out of his hiding place, his sister grabbed the magazine.

"What happened to Silas at the dinner?" she asked.

"He — he got drunk!" replied Tarkington, and then he went on to write that although he tried hard to be a very nonchalant and sophisticated reader, he choked up and had to hurry off to be alone.

This is an engaging picture of the novelist as adolescent — Booth Tarkington still in his Penrod period being moved to tears by Howells's fiction. Howells's impact on Tarkington was a significant factor throughout his career. He never changed his mind about Howells's talent and importance as a novelist. In this same obituary article, Tarkington wrote of Howells: "He knew how to make true things and showed others how to make them." Earlier when Howells wrote Tarkington in 1914 praising *The Turmoil,* Tarkington replied: "Any writer in America would rather have a word from you than from any other man . . . you are responsible for whatever good . . . we produce." Tarkington later told George Ade that Howells was the "only critic alive worth pleasing." Even if we discount these words from a grateful younger writer to a distinguished older one, they still are significant. Tarkington does carry on in American literature the Howells brand of realism — truthful treatment of material, fidelity to the depiction of everyday incident, creation of character we all recognize as normal. Tarkington always felt himself a sort of inheritor of the Howells tradition and was proud to carry it on. When Howells's reputation went into eclipse in the sociological thirties, Tarkington's fame also suffered; but the pendulum has a way of swinging back, and the "beautiful time" that Henry James predicted for Howells may already be here. If so, Tarkington should benefit too.

The bulk of our serious fiction has always been and continues to be written more or less in the realistic mode. This is true despite the contemporary appeal of the fabulators and the creators of currently fashionable metafiction and surfiction. The Nabokovs, Vonneguts, Barthelmes, Pynchons, and Kosinskis may receive more space in the critical journals, but interest in Howells continues strong and is growing. I suspect also that if people would try some of Tarkington's best work they would find him better than they have been led to believe. I tried teaching *The Magnificent Ambersons* in a graduate seminar at the University of California recently, and it was a big success. My students knew of the novel, because the Orson Welles film made from it seems to be revived once in a while on TV in California. They found the novel well worth their time and an appropriate companion for novels by Sherwood Anderson, Edith

Wharton, Willa Cather, and others that we were reading in the same course. It is a pity that *The Magnificent Ambersons* is the only one of the *Growth* trilogy in print — no doubt the Orson Welles influence — but I would like to see both *The Turmoil* and *The Midlander* put out in paperback. In addition, I have been suggesting for some time that publishers reissue *Alice Adams* in a paperback edition — so far unsuccessfully — for I think that novel stands the test of time pretty well. As for other Tarkington titles, I am sorry to say, only *Monsieur Beaucaire* and *Penrod* are available in paperbound editions. Another eight titles are in print in hardcover editions — some pretty expensive — aimed at library sales — and that is it.

To return to Tarkington himself. The fifteen-year-old boy who wept over Silas Lapham's disaster grew up to be a novelist. It wasn't easy, and the road to success was strewn with rejection slips. Tarkington's struggle was not as grim as that of another young man in San Francisco — Jack London — who was trying to get published at about the same time. Tarkington did not have to pawn his bicycle and overcoat and to starve himself as London did, but the frustrations were similar. London thought that New York publishers must have some kind of mechanical monster that opened envelopes and sent back manuscripts without any human involvement. Tarkington's manuscripts came back from New York so fast that he thought there must be someone in Philadelphia intercepting his mail. Fortunately for Tarkington the great man of the family, the uncle for whom he was named, Newton Booth, former governor of California, had died in 1892 and left him a bequest. With this money and free board and room in his parents' house, he was able to survive the lean years of apprenticeship. He recalled in 1900 after *The Gentleman from Indiana* had rocketed him to national prominence: "I was for five years and more one of the rejected — as continuously and successively, I suppose, as anyone who ever wrote."

Early one morning during this period he went for a walk after an unusually long writing session. He met the milkman coming up the walk and stopped to talk:

> "You been up all night?" he [the milkman] asked.
> "Yes," I [Tarkington] answered.
> "What you been doin'?" he went on.
> "Working," said I.
> "Workin'!" said he. "What at?"
> "Writing," said I.
> "How long?" said he.
> "Since yesterday noon," said I. "About sixteen hours."
> "My God," said he. "You must have lots of time to
>   waste!"

If he seemed lazy and self-indulgent to the milkman and the

neighbors, it was appearance only, not reality. In fact he was working very hard to learn his trade. He sometimes bogged down in the sentimental claptrap of the 1890s; and when he began writing his first novel, he made a false start by laying the opening scenes in Bar Harbor, Maine, instead of Indiana where it belonged. Eventually he got the action properly located and the novel completed, but it took five years.

It was not all work, however, during the apprentice years. Tarkington was active in local theatricals, in which he acted as well as wrote plays. And he was very social. He often could be seen racing about Indianapolis in a red-wheeled runabout behind a lively pair of trotting horses. There is a bit of Booth Tarkington in the portrait of young Georgie Minafer of *The Magnificent Ambersons.* Georgie too raced about the city in his runabout, but unlike his creator he was a much-spoiled young man with no interest in doing anything for a career. Tarkington sandwiched his long hours of writing between his hours of partying, but also like Georgie, he was very attractive to women. When I was working on Tarkington's biography in the Princeton Library in 1952, among the mountainous pile of material accumulated from a long lifetime were bundles of old love letters. These were mute testimony to his charm in the 1890s. Most of them, however, were very dull reading half a century later, but one of his old girl friends interested me considerably, a girl named Irma von Starkloff from Saint Louis, who had met Tarkington while visiting a cousin in Indianapolis. She had a lively intelligence, and while she obviously had fallen for Tarkington, the two carried on a literary dialogue. Later I found out that this girl had become Irma Rombauer, the author of *The Joy of Cooking,* and while I was writing my book, I visited her in Saint Louis. She was a spry seventy-five then and reminisced about Tarkington as we sipped scotch on the rocks in her living room. She was appalled to learn that her letters were enshrined in the Princeton Library, but she confirmed all the reports of Tarkington's attractiveness in his apprentice years.

When Tarkington finally finished his novel, eastern publishers did not beat a track to his door. It remained for his indomitable sister Hauté [also spelled *Hautie*], who was by then Mrs. Ovid Butler Jameson, to browbeat S. S. McClure into reading the manuscript. She had great faith in her brother's eventual success and on one of her trips to New York carried along a copy of Tarkington's eighteenth-century costume romance, *Monsieur Beaucaire.* That perennial favorite that once provided a play for Richard Mansfield, movies for Rudolph Valentino and Bob Hope, and reading enjoyment for countless thousands was written before the completion of *The Gentleman from Indiana.* Mrs. Jameson, who had a letter of introduction to McClure, left the manuscript for him to read. When she returned some days later, McClure's partner, John Philips, tried to reject the manuscript. Mrs. Jameson made him confess that McClure had not even read the story and then bullied McClure into reading it. But when McClure did not care for an eighteenth-century romance, Mrs. Jameson told him about the Indiana novel her brother was finishing. McClure, who grew up in Illinois after emigrating from Ireland, thought he would like to examine a manuscript about a crusading small-town Hoosier newspaper editor. Mrs. Jameson wired her brother to rush the manuscript to New York.

Tarkington sent it off without much hope. His sister was the perennial optimist. He expected it to come back as all the rest of his fiction had. You can imagine his shocked surprise when he received a letter a couple of weeks later from Hamlin Garland, who then was at the peak of his literary success. The letter began: "Mr. McClure has given me your manuscript, *The Gentleman from Indiana,* to read. You are a novelist." Tarkington never forgot that letter, which, as he remembered, "changed everything for me," with its four dumbfounding words: "You are a novelist." And so he was. By the time he died forty-seven years later, he had produced over forty volumes of prose fiction, won two Pulitzer Prizes, and achieved a respectable place for himself in the history of American letters.

I find it interesting and appropriate that Garland should have been the reader that McClure turned to for advice. Garland was a Howells protégé, and in 1891 when Garland's own *Main-Travelled Roads* had appeared, Howells had given it a send-off by writing a handsome introduction. Garland too had grown up in the Midwest — in Iowa — and had made his reputation by writing realistic stories of Midwest farm life. Thus Tarkington's story of rural Indiana found an interested reader. Then, too, the Howells connection has another interesting aspect: Howells himself had come out of the Midwest and had succeeded in working his way into the Eastern literary establishment.

Howells, however, did not discover Tarkington in 1899. *The Gentleman from Indiana* had too much sentimental romance in it for his taste and was only partially realistic. When Howells visited Indianapolis on a lecture tour in 1899 after Tarkington's novel had come out, he had little to say about the book. Even though he was taken to dinner at Mrs. Jameson's house where he dined with Tarkington and ex-President Benjamin Harrison, he merely said, when asked by a reporter, that he had read the novel with pleasure. He added that Tarkington was a novelist of great promise, but his remarks seem in retrospect more a gracious gesture than a conviction. Howells restrained his enthusiasm until Tarkington hit his stride with the first of the *Growth* trilogy. Then the praise was unstinting; it was a sort of laying on of hands.

That dumbfounding letter from Garland was followed immediately by a business letter from McClure, who not only wanted to publish the novel in book form but also to serialize it in his magazine. For the purposes of the magazine, however, the manuscript would have to be cut drastically, and McClure invited Tarkington to come East to do it. Tarkington lost no time in getting to New York, and from the moment he walked into McClure's office, he found himself surrounded by editors and writers falling all over themselves to be cordial. He met Garland and F. N. Doubleday that first morning in McClure's office, and as McClure introduced him to the famous journalist Ida Tarbell, the publisher said: "This is to be the most famous young man in America." McClure was given to hyperbole and uninhibited enthusiasm for the writers he discovered, and we have to discount his words somewhat, but Tarkington was indeed no longer to be an obscure young man from the provinces. For the rest of his life he occupied a prominent place in the American literary world. And it must be said that McClure had a good track record for discovering talent. For example, just four years later an obscure high school English teacher in Pittsburgh, who had sent a manuscript to McClure, received a telegram summoning her to New York to discuss publishing her first work of fiction. That was the real beginning of Willa Cather's literary career.

A few days after Tarkington arrived in New York, McClure took him to his home on the south shore of Long Island and installed him in a guest room so that he could carry out the surgical procedures necessary to prepare *The Gentleman from Indiana* for the serial version. Tarkington lived in a perpetual state of excitement as he made the cuts, wrote connecting links, and waited for the typist to retype the manuscript. McClure overwhelmed him with hospitality, offered him a job on the magazine, and solicited his company on a trip to Europe the next summer. He resisted these blandishments, however, and after a marvelous three months in New York returned to Indianapolis in May 1899, as the novel began its serialization. His career was well launched, and the following year McClure brought out in book form *Monsieur Beaucaire* after serializing it in the magazine in December and January. Thus within a year the "most famous young man in America" had two best-sellers making the cash registers ring in bookstores throughout the land.

I now skip over the next three years of Tarkington's life which included two more novels and his foray into Indiana politics. The legislative experience resulted in some interesting political stories published in 1905 as *In the Arena,* but what I want to talk about next is a personal relationship that became extremely significant some ten years later. This was the relationship between Tarkington and his sister's children. Booth Tarkington had a genius for being an uncle, and the three Jameson boys, who ranged in ages from one to fourteen at the time I am speaking of, were always a source of interest to their uncle. Their relationship first comes to our attention during Tarkington's grand tour of Europe in 1903–04, which he made with his wife and parents. During the trip he wrote frequent letters home to John and Donald, the two older nephews. These letters were published after his death under the title *Your Amiable Uncle*. He illustrated them with his own drawings, and they are still amusing to read. They are witty, satiric, and above all entertaining; the avuncular interest is clear in every one. Some examples: from Paris on October 12, 1903, he wrote: "We are buying Xmas presents for you — they have such wonderful things here; and we have bought you each a lovely, calf-bound hymnal. You will be *mad* with joy. But that is not all. Perhaps I shouldn't tell you, so far ahead — it may spoil half your pleasure in getting them, but I can't resist. Each of you is to have a fine woodcut engraving of the Apostle Peter." A few days later from Switzerland Tarkington sent Donald Jameson (then twelve) a postcard and wrote on it: "This is where William Tell lived. I bought the apple shot off his son's head, but I thoughtlessly left it in my room. Papa John [Tarkington's father] came in and ate it, not knowing it wasn't an ordinary apple." Still later after Tarkington had traveled by train from Venice to Florence, he wrote the Jameson boys about some of the people in their compartment on the train. "We had four boys of your age in that compartment; but much better educated than you are, because they spoke Italian fluently. It ought to make you ashamed — we saw children of four in Paris who spoke French. It made me feel that my nephews are an idle, worthless lot." On other occasions he continued the joking about gifts, and from Capri he wrote that among the presents now on hand for the nephews were a "handsome big doormat with 'Wipe Your Feet' in large, attractive letters . . . a splendid edition of *Lives of the Saints*," and embroidered mottoes such as "Home Sweet Home," "Virtue Is Its Own Reward," and "Honor Thy Uncle." This interest in his nephews flowered a decade later when Tarkington began writing the Penrod stories.

Before I take up these stories, however, I need to summarize the decade between the grand tour of 1903–04 and the invention of Penrod Scofield. During the rest of the first decade of this century, Tarkington lived a peripatetic life as novelist, playwright, and expatriate. The trip to Europe with his wife and parents led to more European travel, long stays abroad, and the literary use of his foreign experiences. His playwriting often kept him in New York where he lived out of a suitcase, drank, smoked, and played too much. The antics of his Kokomo lawyer in *The Man from Home*, the play that he wrote with Harry Leon Wilson, were a tremendous box office success, but this period in his life was generally unproductive and very unstable. Its products were not vintage Tarkington. By 1911 he was fast killing himself with alcohol, and before the year was out his marriage went sour and ended in divorce.

Tarkington's life breaks sharply on the sixteenth of January 1912. This was the day he swore off liquor and started both a physical and spiritual recovery. By the end of that year, he had progressed so far that he managed to persuade Susanah Robinson of Dayton to marry him. His second marriage turned out to be a great success, a warm and fulfilling relationship that lasted for the rest of his life. Happily married, Tarkington then settled down in Indianapolis with Susanah and began writing the novels and stories that mark the major phase of his literary career. During the next decade, he produced one after another: *The Flirt, Penrod, The Turmoil, Seventeen, Penrod and Sam, The Magnificent Ambersons,* and *Alice Adams.* He also returned to playwriting and wrote his best play, *Clarence,* the vehicle that launched Alfred Lunt on his distinguished career and provided Helen Hayes with one of her first adult roles.

The first important result of his happy second marriage and his renewed creative energy was *The Flirt.* This is a flawed novel, but it is an important one because in it Tarkington finally found his flood subject — middle-class, urban, Midwestern life. *The Flirt* is his first Indianapolis novel, and the title character, Cora Madison, is the best fictional creation Tarkington had yet produced. The novel also has a significant boy character in Cora's bumptious younger brother, Hedrick. Three months after *The Flirt* was published, Hedrick's avatar appeared as Penrod in his sawdust box in the stable behind the Scofield house.

Susanah Tarkington, whose love and efficiency created a productive environment for her writer-husband, played a seminal part in the creation of *Penrod.* She had been reading a novel dealing with boy life at the English public school Harrow and had been moved by the suffering the small boys went through during hazing by the older lads. She gave the book to her husband to read and was much surprised when he reacted unfavorably. He admitted that the hazing was probably authentic, but he complained that no boys — not even English boys at a public school — ever talked like the children in that novel. Susanah then challenged him to write about boys as they really were. Well, he thought maybe he would, and he disappeared into his workroom for two or three weeks of concentrated effort. He would not discuss what he was writing until one day he called Susanah and read her the first of the Penrod stories, "Penrod and the Pageant." This tale, which appeared in June 1913, in *Everybody's Magazine,* ultimately grew into the book *Penrod,* an American classic of boy life.

The Penrod stories are compounded from several sources. First of all was Tarkington's own memory of boyhood, his growing up in the old homestead at 1100 North Pennsylvania. The initial story of Penrod and the pageant was drawn from his youthful suffering as a pinned, powdered, bewigged, and involuntary actor in charity entertainments gotten up by his older sister Hauté. He too had been the child Sir Launcelot in tights made from old silk stockings, trunks fashioned from wornout red flannel underwears, and a doublet created from a discarded dress. Tarkington also remembered and used the distasteful dancing classes he had been made to attend as a boy, the annual visit of the circus, the feud with his fourth grade teacher, shows staged in the stable loft, and the narratives he wrote as a schoolboy.

When the well of his own memories ran dry, he remembered or watched the antics of his nephews. In the early years of his literary career, Tarkington had had under his daily observation the play of John and Donald Jameson, who lived across the street and were just the ages of Penrod Scofield and Sam Williams. Finally, in 1913 when he actually began writing the stories, John Jameson was out of college and Donald was a senior at Princeton; but Booth Jameson, born in 1902, was just Penrod's age, and every day Uncle Booth watched the neighborhood children playing in the old stable that still survived behind the house. On one occasion he asked Booth Jameson what he thought of a particular neighborhood lad who seemed from observation somewhat more civilized than the rest of the boys. "We call him the little gentleman," replied young Booth, and from that youthful epithet was born Georgie Bassett, the model boy whose impeccable behavior is a continual reproach to Penrod. The Penrod stories are in essence, to use Henry James's phrase, "a direct impression of life." Tarkington himself commented later when the stories were being dramatized: "I know what makes Penrod because I've been years on the job."

The genre to which *Penrod* belongs is the realistic boy story, which had a well-rooted tradition in American literature by 1913. Tarkington traced the type back to Mark Twain, who created the first boy story, as Tarkington put it, in which "the hero was recognizable *as a boy* throughout the whole narrative." Until *Tom Sawyer* was written, he added, "nearly all the boys of fiction were adults with a lisp, or saintly infants, or mischievous eccentrics or merely the sturdy 'young gentlemen' who fought with the butcher's boy before going to Eton in the English novels." William Allen White's Boyville stories (1899) and Stephen Crane's *Whilomville Stories* (1900) continued the tradition; and after Tarkington added his distinguished contribution to this genre, the tradition was continued briefly by F. Scott Fitzgerald with his Basil Duke Lee stories that reflect a strong Tarkington influence and more recently in the stories and the novel, *The Catcher in the Rye,* of J. D. Salinger.

Tarkington had firm ideas of what boy life was really like and relegated to the limbo of bogus literary works most stories of childhood. Thomas Hughes's British novel, *Tom Brown's Schooldays,* and its American counterpart, Thomas Bailey Aldrich's *The Story of a Bad Boy,* were two of the phony ones. In both of these novels, at the appropriate moment the hero thrashes the bully and virtue triumphs in good didactic fashion. Tarkington believed that kids were little savages who had to be civilized by relentless parental and societal pressures. The bully Rupe Collins gets beaten up in *Penrod* by Penrod's black playmates, Herman and Verman, but the boys do not play by any Marquis of Queensberry rules. They go after their adversary with a variety of garden implements, and Rupe Collins is lucky he does not get killed.

The differences between *Tom Sawyer* and *Penrod* are instructive. Although Tarkington believed the real boy story stemmed from Mark Twain, the Penrod stories are quite unlike Twain's book. "Tom and Huck [Finn]," wrote Tarkington, "are realistic only in character. He [Twain] gave 'em what boys don't get when it came to 'plot.' All that the boy, Sam [Clemens], had wished to happen, he made happen." Penrod doesn't find buried treasure, run away from home, and then sneak back to watch his own funeral, or get lost in a cave — these are exceptional adventures. Penrod's escapades are the sort of stuff that boy life is really made of — but Tarkington does allow Penrod to have the last word. Most of Penrod's effects are subdued, and the book succeeds through the abundant use of accurately observed detail. "The detail — *not plot* — is what has made it," wrote Tarkington to George Tyler when the latter wanted to have the stories dramatized. The Penrod stories were not written for children, any more than were Twain's book and Stephen Crane's tales. It's Penrod's suffering and his mental processes, not what happens to him, that adults enjoy.

When Tarkington remarried and settled down in Indianapolis after eight years of wandering, he found that his roots still were deeply planted in the Midwest. He felt unexpected stirrings as he began to survey his hometown as the source of fiction. For the rest of his life he regarded himself as a resident Hoosier, even after he built a summer home at Kennebunkport, Maine, and spent more than half the year there. He always came back to Indiana for the winter, and while he admitted he liked Maine better than Indiana, Indianapolis, he exclaimed, "is sort of a *person* — my uncle or somebody." But long residence in the East and abroad gave him perspective on the Midwest and brought into sharp focus the contrasts between Indianapolis at the turn of the century and on the eve of World War I. And when he thought of the city of his youth, the differences were even more astonishing. Indianapolis had grown from an oversized country town to become a good-sized industrial city. The self-contained society that he remembered had crumbled before the growing complexities of a polyglot urban population. To make the contrast even more startling — and depressing — the natural gas that had fueled the furnaces of central Indiana at the beginning of the century had run out and been replaced by soft coal. Dirt, grime, soot were everywhere, and to one who lived at 1100 North Pennsylvania, there was no getting away from the soft coal smoke.

After two years back in Indiana, Tarkington wrote the first of his *Growth* trilogy, *The Turmoil,* in which he indicts business, the pursuit of wealth, and the mindless advocacy of physical growth. Smoke is the dominant symbol of the novel, and the monstrous industrial complex that spews it out seems to repeat this refrain: "Wealth! I will get Wealth! I will make Wealth! I will sell Wealth for more Wealth! I shall be dirty, my garment shall be dirty, and I will foul my neighbor so that he cannot be clean — but I will get Wealth!" Tarkington wrote to a friend while his novel was being serialized: "Commercialism is the savage of the world; it's that stinking brute I'm after . . . in *The Turmoil,* which is written much more feebly than I'd like." Despite his disclaimer, however, it is a strong story and makes interesting reading in the ecological 1980s. A few years ago I wrote an introduction to a new edition of this novel at the request of a professor of engineering who was working up materials to support courses in environmental studies. The novel is well suited for this extrinsic purpose. It depicts dramatically a period in our history when haste, waste, and insensitivity to social problems had few opponents. When the self-made millionaire James Sheridan in the novel sees smoke pouring out of smokestacks, he chuckles. As soot falls on his cuff, he smacks his lips and says: "Good, clean soot; it's our life-blood, God bless it!" He saw the smoke as a symbol of his fortune and the growing wealth of the city. When a smoke-abatement committee of women visits him, asking his aid in ridding the city of its blight, he tells them jovially: "Smoke's what brings your husbands' money home on Saturday night."

The Turmoil is the story of an ascending family, first generation makers of the wealth. James Sheridan at the outset of the novel is the owner of the biggest skyscraper, the biggest trust company, and the biggest manufacturing works in the city. Having come from the country in his youth, Sheridan, like Howells's paint manufacturer in *The Rise of Silas Lapham,* has risen to wealth but not to social position. His success in business has not prepared him for success in human relations, and while he possesses a Midas touch, his acquisitive genius is no more able than the fabled king's to buy happiness. The conflicts in the novel arise from his efforts to run his family like a financial and industrial empire. He kills his favorite son as a sacrifice on the altar of business. He dismisses an unacceptable suitor, only to have his daughter elope. He forces a second son into the business and watches the boy crack under the double strain of parental coercion and marital trouble. Sheridan wins his main contest, however, which involves his youngest son, Bibbs, a fragile, poetic young man who wants no part in the family enterprises. Bibbs ultimately suppresses his own desire to write and by an act of will makes himself into the image of his father.

The Sheridans in *The Turmoil* are a composite of many families who rose to positions of affluence and power in the Midwest during the early years of the century. The father is the high priest of Bigness, who all his life has "struggled and conquered, and must all his life go on struggling and inevitably conquering, as part of a vast impulse not his own." He is a convincing character, though his material values and domestic bullheadedness do not inspire affection. Bibbs also is a real creation, as Howells wrote appreciatively when the novel began to appear in *Harper's*. He recalls something of Tarkington's own attractiveness during the 1890s, and under different circumstances Tarkington himself might have lived the part he made for Bibbs.

Bibb's compensation for having to go into the family business is a charming heroine, Mary Vertrees, who is the daughter of a declining old family; and this linking of the *nouveau riche* with the old aristocracy provides the material for Tarkington's next volume in the *Growth* trilogy, *The Magnificent Ambersons*. This novel is perhaps too well known to need further discussion, but it brought Tarkington his first Pulitzer Prize; and it depicts vividly the other side of the coin — the slow disintegration of the Amberson fortune through the onslaught of modern growth. At the end of the novel, the spoiled Georgie Minafer swallows his pride and goes to work to make a place for himself in the new era; and the cycle that Howells had described in the fortunes of the Boston Corey family in *The Rise of Silas Lapham* is once more repeated in midland American society.

After *The Magnificent Ambersons* appeared, Indianapolis residents made a parlor game out of matching up the fictional setting to the real history of the city. They figured out the Amberson Addition with its large homes and cast-iron statues had been modeled after Woodruff Place. The Amberson mansion, however, was put in Woodruff Place by artistic license, as Tarkington explained to a *Life* magazine editor in 1942 when Orson Welles was making his movie out of the novel. The actual model was the old Knights of Columbus headquarters on Delaware Street. Of further historic interest too was the character of Eugene Morgan, the pioneer automobile manufacturer, who reminded Indianapolis readers that their city once had rivaled Detroit as a center for making motor vehicles.

Tarkington's marvelous social comedy *Alice Adams* and the third novel in the *Growth* trilogy, *The Midlander,* also are important novels and round out Tarkington's greatest accomplishment in his most fruitful decade. In *Alice Adams* Tarkington returned to social comedy, and while he still was studying social mobility among urban groups, Alice's efforts to catch a rich socially prominent young man end not in tragedy but in pathos. As she climbs the steps of Frincke's Business College to begin learning typing and shorthand, the reader sighs and reminds herself that this is life, not romance, that Alice's fate is after all what happens to most of us. *The Midlander,* the last of the *Growth* trilogy, appeared after a three-year interval, in 1924, and it is a somber story of blasted hopes and unrealized possibilities. Its hero, Dan Oliphant, is a real-estate promoter, a man with a vision of the city beautiful, but he is crushed by the consolidators who take over his financial empire. He dies at the end, lonely and unhappy, a victim of the city's growth.

There is an interesting connection between this novel and Tarkington's own life at this time. One of Dan Oliphant's projects in the novel is the development of a new subdivision on the outskirts of the city in the area north of Thirty-eighth Street. It was into this section of the city that Tarkington was about to move himself, and in the same year the *The Midlander* was published, he bought a house at 4270 North Meridian. He lived in that house the rest of his life. Leaving the old home at 1100 North Pennsylvania, however, caused a pang, but he wasn't sorry to leave the smoke and dirt. The commercial center of the city long since had encroached on the old homestead, and North Meridian Street was then like living in the country. The house he bought, a half-timbered house constructed in the Tudor style, had been built eleven years earlier or just about the time his fictional Dan Oliphant was building houses in his Ornaby Addition. The house stood on a beautiful lot covered with trees — some of them the original forest trees — and both of the Tarkingtons were enchanted with their surroundings.

The year after moving into the new house, the Tarkingtons made a long trip to Europe, then settled down to what Booth called his milk run — up to Maine in the spring and back to Indiana in the winter. He soon began to develop cataracts and was blind for a period, after which he underwent several operations at Johns Hopkins. He regained partial sight, but his physical vigor was diminished in his final years.

After the return of his sight, Tarkington plunged into art collecting on a substantial scale. His interest in art began in his youth with some modest acquisitions, but by the thirties he was turning his avocation into literary material. The stories he wrote for the *Saturday Evening Post* about the art business were collected into a very entertaining book, *Rumbin Galleries* (1937), and he went on to write a book about his own collection, *Some Old Portraits* (1939). The inspiration for the latter volume was his delight at the vivid colors he could see following his operations. Gone was the gray world of the cataract sufferer, and the paintings he already owned took on subtleties of texture and tone that he never had noticed before.

When the bottom dropped out of the art market during the Great Depression, Tarkington's income dipped only slightly. He was able to afford an impressive number of paintings by Reynolds, Gainsborough, Lawrence, Lely, Stuart, and others — even a Titian, a Velásquez, and a Goya. He wrote a friend that he was buying pictures instead of stocks and argued that they were more depression-proof than securities. The paintings that he gathered about him during the last decade of his life provided endless enjoyment. *Some Old Portraits* is a charming book that reflects this pleasure, but it is more than that. As his friend, the art historian Erwin Panofsky, said, it was a book "the like of which no art historian could ever write — a book that compels the painter to tell us more about human nature than he reveals in the picture, and compels the sitter to tell us more about human nature than he revealed to the painter."

The last eight years of Tarkington's life were spent quietly — winters in Indianapolis and summers at Kennebunkport, Maine. He continued to work, as the habits of a lifetime did not desert him, and he wrote five more novels between 1939 and his death seven years later. He enjoyed the company of his neighbor Kenneth Roberts during his summers in Maine and served as advisor and critic for Roberts's historical fiction. In the winters in Indianapolis, he entertained old friends like the Lunts, Alexander Woollcott, and Helen Hayes and took pleasure in the company of his nephews and nieces, as well as his grandnephews and grandnieces. Performances of the Indianapolis Symphony and recordings of classical music brightened his final years. He remained a *bon vivant* and witty raconteur, as Susanah Mayberry's memoir demonstrates, until the end, and when he died in 1946, he had lived a full, satisfying, and fulfilled life.

The author of this book and her uncle about the time she first became aware of his colorful presence.

RECOLLECTIONS

SMALL CHILDREN ARE MORE AWARE THAN ADULTS GIVE them credit for being. When I was five or six, from among the blur of forms that made up my large family, one figure emerged whose outline was strong — and he was special to me. This man created an ambience of anticipation. When he was present, he colored my ordinary small-child's world with fun and excitement. Although he was a grown-up — and an old grown-up at that — I was drawn to him as a filing is to a magnet. His name? Booth Tarkington. At that early age, I was not conscious of the details of his appearance or voice, but later memories are vivid.

When I became really conscious of his existence, he was at the height of his career as novelist and dramatist, but to my generation of his family, he was first and always Uncle Booth. By 1921, the year I was born, he had written sixteen best-sellers and many plays. Although he had twice won the Pulitzer Prize — with *The Magnificent Ambersons* in 1919 and *Alice Adams* in 1922 — the fact that he was one of the most popular American writers of the early twentieth century completely escaped me as I was growing up.

In his autobiography, *As I Seem to Me,* written for the *Saturday Evening Post* in 1941 (it was never published in book form), Uncle Booth said, "Our family possessed, besides worthy ancestors, a living Great Man; and, like other families that have this privilege, we borrowed greatness from our hero."[1] He was referring to his uncle Newton Booth, one of the first post-Civil War governors of California. Our generation, too, had its Great Man. It was Booth Tarkington, and I, at least, certainly "borrowed greatness" from him.

My egoism was fertilized by the sure knowledge that six of his books were dedicated to me, his great-niece. I have the good fortune to be named after his second wife, Susanah, and it never once occurred to me during my early childhood that his dedications were meant for her. As a child I never read beyond the dedication page, but I was not too little to be able to read on it "To Susanah," my own name. If I once or twice wondered whether we really knew each other well enough for him to give me this honor, I never asked anyone about it; and in some mysterious way, I thought it reflected credit on me. I never even thought of his books as especially important. Our bookshelves were filled with autographed copies and first editions of Tarkington, but for me he was not a writer per se. He was Uncle Booth, the most important and exciting person in my life.

◆ ◆ ◆ ◆ ◆ ◆ ◆ ◆ ◆

TO MY SURPRISE WHEN I WAS YOUNG, I CAME TO REALIZE that Uncle Booth had not lived in a vacuum waiting until I was born. His earlier years had been busy ones. A first glance at his autobiography reveals an ordinary childhood, but closer reading uncovers hilarious escapades. Some of them appear in *Penrod.* Before he could write, he dictated stories to his sister, Hautie (my grandmother, whose name was spelled *Hauté,* also). He gave elaborate shows in the stable, one being "Jessie James in 14 Acts." And once at a party, he jumped out of the window to avoid kissing games, then learned to his chagrin that no one had missed him.

When in high school, he played hooky for more than two months. During his truancy, he presented a cheerful face to his parents as he lied about school activities. He wrote in his autobiography: "Except those most concerned — the members of my family and the high school authorities — everybody of my acquaintance came to have knowledge of the dreadful prodigy. . . . and, in many a hurriedly withdrawn glance at my face, I read that I was regarded as the hero of a fearsome exploit. Glances like that flicker in the death house."[2]

When his crime was discovered, his parents did not even make him go back to school. All they said to him was "Oh, Booth," and sent him East to Phillips Exeter Academy in the following fall, 1887 — something they could ill afford to do. According to Uncle Booth, his time at Exeter was disastrous: "I had no consciousness of any hour but the present; whatever was idiotic engrossed me,"[3] he ran up huge bills he could not pay and stayed at school the summer following graduation in 1889 to work on the class yearbook, the other editors having decamped. He ignored anxious letters from his parents telling him of his grandmother's serious illness and her wish to see him. She died before he got home.

Months after his return, his father spoke to him just once about his profligacy. Father and son were sitting outdoors one summer evening:

> *"Oh, Booth ——" he said, and paused.*
> *"Yes, sir?" . . .*
> *"I thought you might like to know . . . I got the last of those bills of yours paid today."*
> *In my room that night I didn't read; I didn't light the gas.*
> *. . . Never afterward did I contract a debt that I didn't know I could pay. I seem to have been one of those who improve only through punishment; yet the thought doesn't discourage me. Whole nations are like that.*[4]

Uncle Booth took an enforced sabbatical between Exeter and college because of straitened family finances. Then in August of 1890, he went to visit at Maxinkuckee in northern Indiana, where his spirits were enlivened by his meeting with Geneve Reynolds. They played tennis and argued "spiritedly" about Robert Browning and George Meredith. She dismissed his opinions with "satirical gaiety," but he had to see more of her. After the vacation she returned to her home in Lafayette, Indiana. Uncle Booth immediately found out that at Purdue University, located across the Wabash River from Lafayette, was a professor who taught pen-and-ink drawing. He fervidly told his puzzled parents he *had* to study under the great Prof. Ernest Knaufft. Nowhere else could he learn craftmanship "in the linear art." His only reason for going to Purdue in 1890 was so he could continue his discussion of writers with Geneve. Alas, he had no sooner enrolled as a student than he found out that many other males wanted to talk to her, too, most of them unmarried professors and instructors. The competition was too stiff, and it seemed "disadvantageous" to try to talk to the young lady when his own faculty wished her company. He wrote: "Despondent, I sometimes devoted myself to the curriculum and even slightly, to athletics."[5] He had an 89 average in his academic subjects and wrote for the *Lafayette Sunday Times* and the *Purdue Exponent.* He was delighted to have opportunities to talk with two recent graduates, George Ade and John McCutcheon, who, he said, "were brilliancies out of another world and long evenings with them were amelioration for what I suffered from professional and other rivals."[6] Eventually Geneve's engagement was announced to a member of the board of trustees.

Uncle Booth entered Princeton University in the following fall as a junior. His father wrote to some cousins in New Jersey asking them to keep an eye on his son, adding that the new student would be "devoting himself to journalistic art, or something of that indefinitive mode of procedure toward the poorhouse."[7] He was not able to enroll for a degree because he lacked the necessary credits in classical languages. His uncle Newton Booth, the "celebrity" of Uncle Booth's generation, had gone to California with the 1849 Gold Rush and had become rich by opening a grocery store instead of looking for gold. Since Greek and Latin had not been useful in his frontier life, he had written his sister (Uncle Booth's mother) that Booth should avoid the classics during his education.

While he was at Princeton, Uncle Booth founded the Triangle Club, a dramatic society. In 1893 he wrote, directed, and played the lead in *The Honorable Julius Caesar.* In later years the club began to tour the country during the Christmas vacation and achieved national recognition as an "entertaining college musical comedy troupe." With its production in 1981 of *Bold Type,* as the program states, "Triangle has resurrected a fruitful time-honored theatrical partnership. . . . *Bold Type* is our very own musical version of *The Gentleman from Indiana,*" Uncle Booth's first published book (1899). "Once more," the program text continues, "Booth Tarkington is starring in the Triangle show. . . . a ninety-year reunion taking place under the lights of the stage."[8]

A person of high spirit, Uncle Booth sang, played, drank, and acted his way through the university, achieving good grades without studying and making friendships he cherished all his life. In addition, he wrote for the literary publications, the *Tiger* and the *Nassau Literary Review.* Looking back on those happy days, he recalled, "It was always sunshine then."[9] Although he did not receive a degree, he was, is, and always will be known among Princeton men as "BT '93."

Having given not a thought to the future during those frivolous years, he arrived home as an unemployed person in busy Indianapolis.

◆ ◆ ◆ ◆ ◆ ◆ ◆ ◆ ◆

Oval inset above: *Uncle Newton Booth became governor of California and had a strong influence on Tarkington's family.* Above: (right) *Young Tarkington posing with his cousin* (left) *Fenton Booth and sister, Hautie.* Left: *Tarkington at twenty-eight when he was living at the family home on Pennsylvania Street in Indianapolis while honing his writing skills.*

Above: *The cast of* The Honorable Julius Caesar, *a play written, directed, and acted in by Tarkington* (circled) *and presented in 1893 by the Triangle Club of Princeton University.* Left: *Hautie in about 1899 when she persuaded publisher S. S. McClure to consider her brother's* The Gentleman from Indiana, *the novel which launched Tarkington's career.*

UNCLE BOOTH SAID IN HIS AUTOBIOGRAPHY THAT although he was not ambitious after Princeton, he did yearn to draw. He began to draw in earnest and to write a novel at the same time. *Life,* a pictorial magazine of gentle social satire published by John Ames Mitchell, accepted one of his drawings, but his novel, he said, "banged its head into a stone wall." He could not finish it. He began to strain and fight with writing — without the benefit of anyone's advice or criticism. As he said, "Printed rejection slips clarify only one point."[10] His total gross return for five years of work was $22.50.

"Writing," he stated once, "is a trade and like any other trade it must be learned. There are no teachers. We must learn by failure and by repeated efforts how the thing should be done."[11] A small legacy from his uncle Newton Booth permitted him to spend almost his entire time writing (and being rejected). He thought that his family was heroic about him and that "their embarrassment must have been severe," especially when a great friend of his father referred to him as "'one of these damn literary fellers.'"[12]

During those early years of apprenticeship, Uncle Booth wrote a short novel, *Monsieur Beaucaire,* which met with the usual rejection, so he put the manuscript away. It was, however, *Beaucaire* and my grandmother who made up the vanguard for *The Gentleman from Indiana,* my uncle's first literary success. My grandmother was Uncle Booth's older sister, whom her grandchildren called Nana and everyone else called Hautie. Her foray into the office of S. S. McClure, editor of *McClure's Magazine,* has become a family legend, which I relate from my own memories of her and comments made to me by those people in the family who loved her very much — and some who did not love her at all.

Everyone who has ever known her agrees that Hautie's small frame contained the force of a juggernaut. In 1898 armed with a letter of introduction to McClure and a copy of *Beaucaire* (obtained without the author's knowledge), she — by sheer force of will — induced the editor to read the work. In doing so, she acted completely in character, displaying optimism, patience, determination, charm, guile, and indomitability. All through her life when she undertook a project, for good or ill, she saw it through, although hell or another person should bar the way. Nana left the letter and the manuscript at the office of the magazine and returned a few days later to learn the novel's fate. In an innocent manner, she asked the tired editor assigned to the work if he had enjoyed the poetic quotations at the beginning of each chapter. When he replied that he had indeed enjoyed them very much, she snapped, "There aren't any. Where is Mr. McClure?" Then she sat "like patience on a monument" while McClure did what she had intended him to in the first place. The radicals who staged sit-ins in the sixties and early seventies could have taken lessons from my grandmother.

I have mentioned her patience. In addition, the word *failure* was not admitted to her lexicon. While her sons, John and Donald, disrupted McClure's outer office by spitting water from the fountain at each other (the word *discipline* was not in her lexicon either), a literary career was being launched in the inner office. However, capitulation was not immediate. McClure was not impressed with *Beaucaire*. But Nana had put her size three foot firmly in the door and had no intention of moving it. Using her persuasive powers, which were considerable, she insisted sweetly that he also read *The Gentleman from Indiana*. Her bemused target agreed to do so. She wired Uncle Booth to send the second manuscript immediately, and he did so "dispiritedly."

Several weeks later to his "wondering incredulity" my uncle was told that McClure liked the *Gentleman* very much and wanted to serialize it. (The editor's capitulation to my grandmother greatly increased the sales of *McClure's Magazine*.) Beyond his delight at the book's prospects and his gratitude to his sister for her support, Uncle Booth was exultant for his parents' sake because "they'd always been, touchingly, more interested in my work itself than in its acceptance."[13]

In January 1899 Uncle Booth, like Alice, must have passed through the looking-glass. He left for New York and association with other writers, as well as with the great and near great in the publishing world. What must have been his feelings as he boarded that train — excitement, apprehension, hope, exhilaration? How do we feel when a dream comes true? Maybe the emotions he felt evade description. He had labored long for this day and his reward was at hand. Small wonder that Uncle Booth was always devoted to his sister.

The reason for the trip was to work with McClure on serializing *The Gentleman from Indiana*. We can judge from his letter home after their first meeting that he was given the red-carpet treatment. According to Uncle Booth's letter of February 1, 1899, McClure had told him that for publication in the magazine the novel would be reduced to 60,000 words and, further, "we are going to push you and make you known everywhere — you are to be the greatest of the new generation." Just imagine what the young author must have felt at *those* words! McClure concluded his letter, "You've got a great sister. . . . She took me all of a heap I'll tell you!"[14]

Uncle Booth's letters about his time in New York are exuberant. He was immensely stimulated by the people he met who were at home in the literary world. He wrote his mother that they were "so suggestive, so electric." He put off his return home and explained that he needed the appreciation, interest, and advice of his new friends. In one letter, he announced forthrightly, "The work must be done here."[15]

When he did come home in the spring of 1899, he was no longer the unknown writer from the hinterlands, but he was far from being a hit in Indianapolis. People who had read the two installments of *The Gentleman from Indiana,* which had appeared in *McClure's* before Uncle Booth returned home, thought it held the state up to ridicule. He was even stopped on the street and reviled.

After a few more installments had been published, he wrote that the anger against him calmed down: "They [the readers] perceived that I'd tried, however ineptly, not to knock down but to set up. . . . When the book appeared . . . it was received with a friendly indulgence."[16]

♦ ♦ ♦ ♦ ♦ ♦ ♦ ♦ ♦

UNCLE BOOTH DID NOT LOOK BACK. HE NEVER AGAIN lived full time in Indianapolis. For most of the rest of his life, he wintered there and summered in Kennebunkport, Maine. Much of his young adulthood, however, was spent in New York and traveling on the Continent.

Many stories of his gay young bachelor days (from about 1894 until his first marriage in 1902) have become family lore. His capacity for liquor was fabled. He drank, he said, because it made him happy. During that time he made himself unpopular with a few young wives whose husbands habitually dropped by the University Club in Indianapolis for a drink on their way home from work. If Uncle Booth were there, or, if he came in, he usually locked the door and hid the key. He would then buy drinks for everyone until the bar ran dry — or so the story goes. The husbands arrived home much later and much the worse for wear.

Uncle Booth went to extraordinary lengths to play jokes, although I never heard of anyone being hurt by them. Once in a heavy snowstorm, he took a hansom cab to the University Club in the early evening and asked the driver, an elderly man who often drove him, to wait. Much later, Uncle Booth came out. The driver had taken shelter inside the cab and had fallen deeply asleep. Uncle Booth climbed into the driver's seat and drove the horse back to the cab stand. Then, in the blizzard, he walked to the club, where he called up the driver and raked the poor man over the coals because he had not waited.

Another time while driving through Ohio, Uncle Booth and a friend stopped at every little town on their route to mail an anonymous letter to each mayor. The pranksters were acting on the assumption that every politician has some sort of skeleton in the closet that he wishes to keep there. The letter was brief: "Be very careful! Everything has been discovered. Pack. We will be in touch with you soon." Then they drove on, happy to have given the mayor a jolt.

My father's favorite story about Uncle Booth when he was in his cups involved his passion for fruit stands. Once after a prolonged celebration of the successful Chicago opening of one of his plays, Uncle Booth bought the produce of every fruit stand in the Loop and sent it to his producer. My father delighted in the image of bellboys struggling to carry mounds of fruit down the hotel corridor at 5 A.M. and of the producer's predictable reaction.

Another tale concerns Uncle Booth and two of his friends who were staying at the Algonquin Hotel in New York — fortunately in rooms not too distant from one another. Hearing a knock upon his door, Uncle Booth called, "Come in." His two friends entered, one of them stark naked. The apotheosis of one-upmanship, Uncle Booth looked straight at his nude friend without batting an eye, then asked them both to have a drink. While making plans for the evening, Uncle Booth remained impassive, and the two friends left the room without any recognition from my uncle of the unusual situation. The incident was never mentioned, at least not when Uncle Booth was present.

Uncle Booth told me about one incident that could have ended in violence. He and several friends had been touring the Parisian nightspots and on impulse decided to go into an area of Paris that even *les gendarmes* avoided in the *daytime*. The dregs of criminal lowlife habituated the taverns. He and his friends, dressed in evening clothes, careened into a bar that was the exclusive drinking spot of what Uncle Booth referred to as *les Apaches*. There was suddenly a dead and threatening silence as the men wavered their way to the bar. All the Frenchmen had knives in their waistbands and several, crouching, approached them. Inebriation was instantly replaced by

Oval inset and above respectively: *Tarkington's mother, Elizabeth Booth Tarkington, and father, John S. Tarkington, who were "touchingly, more interested in [their son's] work itself than in its acceptance."* Left: *Mrs. Ovid Butler Jameson — the indomitable Hautie — whose three sons were models for Penrod.*

Left: *The old homestead stood at 1100 Pennsylvania Street in Indianapolis where the boy Booth engaged in antics which the author Booth wove into his Penrod stories.* Below: *Downtown Indianapolis, showing the Soldiers and Sailors Monument on the Circle, as it looked early in the twentieth century when Tarkington served in the Indiana legislature in that city.*

terrified sobriety. Uncle Booth said that he had never been so frightened. The intruders turned to face the attackers, and he was convinced that only one thing saved them. One of his friends had had a bad nosebleed during the evening and his white shirtfront was stained with blood. As the menacing Frenchmen noticed the blood, they grinned evilly, cursed in some kind of patois, and went back to their seats. Uncle Booth and his friends ordered a drink apiece, left them untouched, and silently shivered their way out of the bar, feigning nonchalance, all of them fearing a knife between the shoulder blades. (Contrast this story with the letter quoted later on when he advised me and my college roommate not to go out at night in Boston because the streets were rowdy and street crossings dangerous.)

I read in an obituary for Uncle Booth my own favorite anecdote. I do not know its source, but it sounds typical of my uncle's exploits. The story goes that he and some friends went to Lafayette, Indiana, to see a play by George Ade. After the performance, while refreshing themselves in a bar, they noticed that one of the customers looked very much like Edgar Allan Poe. He was actually the press agent for a road show. He happily and tipsily joined them, and they plied him with liquor. They all ended up in Indianapolis where they put the bewildered gentleman up at the country club. For several days, Uncle Booth and his friends brought naive and flattered guests to see and talk to Poe's impersonator. The fake Poe, prompted by his mentors and whiskey, played the role beautifully during the interviews. The revelers, if they knew, did not pay any attention to the fact that the real Edgar Allan Poe had died nearly fifty years before. The joke could not go on for long. Very soon they bundled him back to Lafayette and to an enraged employer who demanded to know where on earth he had been. "I don't know where I've been or who took me there," he responded, "but I've certainly had one helluva time."

This is not meant to be a homily proclaiming that drinking is fun, but for Uncle Booth it was for a time, at least as far as I know. Of course, it could not have been *all* happy; however, I remember only the funny stories told to me by the older generation in our family.

One story I can tell from my own memory. The incident occurred shortly after World War II, and Uncle Booth had not had a drink for years, although the Tarkingtons always served liquor to their guests. My husband, myself, and a couple our age who were dear friends were invited to the Tarkingtons for a surprise: to sample a gift of a case of Rainwater Madiera from Julian Street, American author and close friend of Uncle Booth. (In 1923 they coauthored *The Country Cousin.*)

There is more than one explanation for the term *Rainwater Madiera,* which is made on the island of Madiera. According to one story, the one I prefer, a shipment of the casks of wine was drenched with rain while lying at dockside in Oporto on the deck of a clipper enroute to Boston. The water leaked into the casks — hence the name *Rainwater.* The new Englanders liked the diluted wine and requested more. Another theory, and probably the correct one, is that the grapes for this wine are grown so high on the hillsides of the island that irrigation is impossible, so the wine is only produced during the years that have sufficient rainfall.

The Madiera was served with walnuts which we cracked ourselves. Uncle Booth was the only one who did not participate in the sipping, and I doubt that anything could have made him. (He claimed that after he stopped drinking altogether a whiff of alcohol smelled like kerosene. I do not know whether I believe this wholly or not, and you can draw your own conclusions.) He warned us not to smoke a cigarette before tasting the wine because tobacco would dull our taste buds. And what did *I* do? I lit a cigarette. Such an inexcusable display of bad manners still makes me cringe. I do not even know why I did it. Whatever the motive, it was ill-bred and impolite, to say the least. Uncle Booth never stopped twinkling at me. In fact he began to grin. I hurriedly squashed out the cigarette as the wine was served, but the smoke from it spiraled lazily upward and smelled terrible. As I fanned the air with my hands, I could see out of the corner of my eye that he had put his hands in front of his mouth, stifling laughter. His delight in a great-niece's pecadilloes was as keen as his pleasure had been in those of her father and uncles. We enjoyed the wine very much (in my case, despite the effects of the cigarette) and thanked him in predictable clichés, having no idea of the treat we had been given. Our palates were used to domestic, drugstore sherry, when we could afford it.

◆ ◆ ◆ ◆ ◆ ◆ ◆ ◆ ◆

IN 1902 UNCLE BOOTH COURTED AND MARRIED LOUISA Fletcher, a young member of one of the prominent banking families of Indianapolis. At first they found each other irresistible. They went to live with Uncle Booth's parents, and the only time they had alone, I think, was when they were residing abroad where they had happy times. Even there his parents and friends joined them for long visits.

All Louisa's contemporaries are dead, but from hearsay among the older generation, I learned there were two schools of thought about her. One was advanced by my father. When I asked him about Louisa, he smiled and made vague curving gestures with his hands, adding that she wore too much perfume. He also said that when she once focused her not inconsiderable charms on one of his Princeton roommates, there was no contest. Others in the family said she was a lovely artistic, sensitive woman, who was no match for her mother-in-law and sister-in-law (the indomitable Hautie). To say that Uncle Booth's feminine relatives were possessive is to understate. My mother has told me many stories about what my grandmother (Hautie again) did to make my mother's life miserable after she married my father.

I have a thin volume of wistful poems that Louisa wrote. She must have been unhappy much of the time and who knows what the real truth was. I am sure that my uncle's fondness for alcohol did not help the situation. I wonder what Uncle Booth did when there was dissension, and there certainly must have been some fireworks. Maybe what many men do — flee — into work or into drink, and the drinking must have been caused to some extent by the family tensions. My grandmother was so powerful and had such a hold on the men in her family that they rarely fought for their beleaguered wives. I think she held "her men" because, despite her occasionally outrageous behavior, she could always entertain them and make them laugh. One woman, though, stood her ground and won hands down, and that was Uncle Booth's second wife, Susanah, of whom more later.

◆ ◆ ◆ ◆ ◆ ◆ ◆ ◆ ◆

DESPITE HIS DIVERTISSEMENTS IN THE LITERARY AND dramatic *haut monde,* Uncle Booth throughout his life was as devoted to members of his family as they were to him. This was clearly shown when as a young man he wrote letters to his nephews while he was traveling in Europe in 1903 and 1904 with Louisa and his parents. He was in high spirits and had appreciative readers among the members of his family at home in Indianapolis.

Still far in the future was *Penrod,* the humorous book for which he is best known, about the very private and eventful life of a boy. But he was already studying the young hellions who were to be its models: Hautie's sons — John, age fourteen; Donald, age twelve; and

Booth, age one — the eldest of whom was my father. In his letters, Uncle Booth addressed his nephews as "Poor Infants," "Angelic Nephews," "Inheritors of Sin," "Most Pious," "O Envious," "Gentlemen of the Guard," and "Share Awfaw," adding that the last salutation was the English pronunciation of *Chers Enfants* and was translated "Wicked Boys."

These letters, delightfully illustrated by the writer with pen-and-ink caricatures in the margins, contain the essence of those qualities that were so much a part of our relationship with him as we grew up. They are breezy and informal, having sentiment without sentimentality and laughter without indignity.

Before my grandmother's death, Uncle Donald rummaged through her desk and found the letters his uncle had written. He put them in the office safe because he and my father (John) suspected one of Hautie's hangers-on of being "sticky-fingered." My father coveted those letters and I am not surprised. He loved Uncle Booth more than he loved almost anyone else in the world. He collected Tarkington first editions — and there in those letters was revealed an uncle known to no one but the immediate family. When they were rediscovered, he must have been thrilled.

But my father was even more thrilled with their appearance in 1949 in the book *Your Amiable Uncle: Letters to His Nephews by Booth Tarkington* (illustrated with his original sketches), which he and David Laurance Chambers edited and which the Bobbs-Merrill Company published. Chambers was the president of that publishing house and a dear friend of Uncle Booth. A limited edition of 1,000 copies was published. If you want a copy today, you must haunt the secondhand bookstores or pay a book-tracing company to search for it — at great expense. My father gave my husband and me one of the first copies of *Your Amiable Uncle* and signed it, "Love, from one of the aimless nephews."

Uncle Booth once wrote of the portrait of a young eighteenth-century Stuart princess that she had the look of a person who knows that any terrible thing may happen at any moment. He, too, knew this very well, but his way of coping with this reality was by filling his own life and the lives of those around him with inspired fun — not the least of which were his lighthearted letters from Europe.

◆ ◆ ◆ ◆ ◆ ◆ ◆ ◆ ◆

From *Your Amiable Uncle*

The following excerpts are from letters Booth Tarkington wrote during his first trip abroad (1903-1904) to his nephews John, Donald, and Booth Jameson. With Tarkington were his first wife, Louisa, and his parents, "Papa John" and "Nana."

Venice
[October 26?]

Dear Infants:

A while ago, as I looked down from our balcony, I saw Papa John and Nana disappearing from the Lagoon into the Grand Canal in a gondola — and it struck me that you would understand my feeling that the sight was quite impossible. I couldn't have imagined it — and seeing it I couldn't believe it! . . .

This afternoon we went to "the Lido," a beach — with hotels, etc. — on the Adriatic, only a couple of hours by gondola, and there, Beneath a Spreading Chestnut Tree, we saw the toughest man in the world. Here he is, without exaggeration. . . .

[Continuation of letter from page 33]

Nana is learning to speak English.
Says it's prettier than Hoosier, but I
don't think so.
Au revoir, mes enfants, soyez les
bons garçons et mangez assez. Je
suis votre aimable
Oncle

Venice
[*October 26?*]

Mes enfants

Appended you will find a faithful
sketch of your relatives at the table
d'hôte this evening. (That doesn't
mean Table d'Hauté.) The puzzle is
to find Nana. It was her *glass, too,*
and it was not all water. . . .

Florence
Oct. 29

Angelic Nephews:

Robin [the family dog] *will weep*
when his mistress [Nana] *returns —*
for he may never hope to see her
face again. She and Papa John have
gone about looking at ceiling fres-
coes so much that the attitude has
become permanent. It is not that
they are haughty, though it does
look so. . . .

Rome
November 1, 1903

My Well-Behaved Nephews:

This is the crowd one used to find at the Colosseum, which was once the Show Grounds here. But things have changed a good deal. All the old gang seem to have disappeared, and nowadays it's like this.

The above pirate with the umbrella is our guide. . . .

Rome
November 3

Dear Nephews:

This is not a copy of an old picture. It is a bad sketch of one of the Papal Guard. He (and half-a-dozen like him) were lounging about the entrance to the Vatican when we went in. . . . They make you think you've suddenly dropped back to The Prince and the Pauper *times. . . .*

The Throwing of Septus.

Rome
November 7

Gifted Ones:

. . . This afternoon we visited, amongst other things, the Tarpeian Rock. This is a cliff of the Capitoline hill. . . . When a Roman did anything his fellow citizens didn't like, they forced him to throw himself, or else threw him, from the Tarpeian Rock. . . .

Rome
Nov. 5th, 1903

Inheritors of Sin:

. . . Below is an Italian mover we saw on the Quirinal hill. The donkeys go up and down the hills with grotesque loads; they look like rabbits hitched to houses. . . .

Naples
Nov. 14-

Dear Nephews:

Here is a scene of this evening; the Neapolitan singers and how the English listened. Papa John will tell you about it. My ink is giving out — —

Capri
December 4, 1903

Most Puissant:

On the next page you will find a picture of Mr. Elihu Vedder, the American painter. He has lived in Rome for thirty years, but is building a villa here. . . . The villa would have upset your ma: Moorish towers, colonnades, arched ceilings, gardens up-stairs, terraces olive orchard and columned arbors. . . .

Capri
Nov. 29

Signori:

You wouldn't expect to see anything like this, allowed to run loose, any-where, would you? But it does, here on Capri; it has passed us several times briskly, at dusk. We thought, of course, it was a hermit, a holy man, but it wasn't. It is a German painter, who lives in a handsome villa and has a large — somewhat Mormon — family and a number of disciples. They practice what is called "the re-turn to Nature," that is they wear few clothes and live on fruit and cab-bage and they sell pictures — oddly enough this madman paints very well. . . .

Capri

Dec. 1, 1903

My poor Nephews:

I take my pen in hand, probably for the last time, to give you a record of the closing days of your relatives (according to Nana). For five days the gale has raged — and the island has sprung a leak and is sinking. We have <u>waisted</u> away for lack of food and none of us weighs over 200. Worst of all, Vesuvius is throwing up and erupting and going-on. . . .

Later

We-are-growing-very-weak. Nana exceedingly despondent but still taking a little nourishment at regular intervals, that is: at the table d'hôte. . . .

Midnight

Nothing to live on until breakfast but a dozen chicken sandwiches and a bottle of wine. Hardly think we'll survive. . . . We have eaten the sandwiches and are reduced to living on . . . blue points and broiled lobster, etc! . . .

Later Yet Still

The leak has been discovered to be from a cistern, so there are some chances that we shall weather-the-storm. . . .

Capri

Saturday Dec. 19, '03

Poor little Ones:

This letter will be very short, to make up for the preceding long one. The drawing on the opposite page is your mad, wild G'ther and an Italian Countess. You wouldn't have thought such things possible, a year ago, would you? Yet it took place this afternoon. She danced the tarantella and Papa John danced, too. The fact that they didn't actually dance the tarantella together has nothing to do with the truthful composition of my picture. . . .

Paris

July 3rd, 1904

Dear Hauté —

. . . Your letters indicate that you are sorry to remember me in my going-away skin, bleached and cadaverous. I wouldn't worry about that; I couldn't get the trousers I wore then on my arms now. I don't think I've ever been so well. . . .

UNCLE BOOTH CONTINUED TO WRITE HARD, PLAY HARD, and drink hard, and again, became intensely interested in the theater, this time as a professional. He was one of a very few American writers who successfully made the transition from novels to plays. Billie Burke, Ruth Gordon, Alfred Lunt, Otis Skinner, and Helen Hayes were but a few of the legendary actors who performed in his works.

By choice he wrote comic plays, collaborating with Harry Leon Wilson on eleven plays beginning with *The Guardian* in 1907. (Uncle Booth and Wilson — who later wrote *Ruggles of Red Gap* — supposedly, during a creative moment in Paris, invented the sidecar: lemon juice, Cointreau, and brandy.) Theirs was a happy marriage of talents. According to Uncle Booth, when his coauthor was concentrating on the writing, he wandered absently around and around a pool table, cue in hand, occasionally sighting along it as he sought the muse.

Their most successful play was *The Man from Home,* which they wrote in 1908 in less than a month on the Isle of Capri where they were living with Julian Street. (I do not know whether Louisa was with them or not, but I assume she was.) The play starred William Hodge, ran for five and a half years, and made its producers a great deal of money. Uncle Booth and Wilson who had collected absurd remarks made by Americans on their first trip abroad found the remarks very useful when spoken by the hero of the play, Daniel Vorhees Pike. When he declared, "I wouldn't trade our State Insane Asylum for the worst ruined ruins in Europe," the authors were laughing at him, but forgivingly. The New York critics, though, reproved the authors for attacking European culture, which had never been their intention.

Uncle Booth wrote to his producer, George Tyler, on July 26, 1925, about the popularity of the play:

> *What made the popularity of* The Man from Home? *One of us — the audience — getting sat on by snobs and foreigners of the High Hat type the same way* we think *those High Hats would snub and sit on us, and then turning on 'em, scoring off of 'em, and handing 'em body blows the way we'd* like *to do ourselves if we knew how. Incidentally* seeming *a nice modest feller of the "dry humour" variety . . . this thrown against an exotic background. Old Home Week projected against the Golfo di Napoli. Vice President Dawes in the Vatican. . . .*[17]

Uncle Booth's attitude toward the work of a dramatist was unusual. He believed that the play's author was only a fraction of the team, and when asked by competent professionals to rewrite lines, he gladly acquiesced. Writing novels, he thought, was incredibly more difficult. The work was solitary and the author alone was responsible for his characters' credibility. The advantage, he said repeatedly, was that once conceived the characters were not changed by the "exigencies of staging" over which the author had no control. Playwriting was a happy change of pace about which he was exuberant — fascinated by the various aspects which had to successfully mesh to create successful theater: the actors' talents, staging limitations, abilities and tact of the directors and producers, preferences of a fickle public, and prejudices of the critics.[18]

In 1909 for several months, he and Harry Leon Wilson had four plays running simultaneously in New York: *Springtime, Foreign Exchange, Getting a Polish,* and *Your Humble Servant,* the last starring Otis Skinner; and two on the road: *The Man from Home* and *Cameo Kirby.* Nat Goodwin opened as the lead in *Cameo Kirby,* but was replaced by Dustin Farnum.[19] *The Man from Home* was the only play, however, that played to Standing Room Only.

◆ ◆ ◆ ◆ ◆ ◆ ◆ ◆ ◆

BY 1909 UNCLE BOOTH'S DRINKING WAS NO LONGER solely for conviviality. His marriage was in serious trouble and he returned to Indianapolis. One can only guess at the unhappiness the disintegration of their marriage caused both him and Louisa. The divorce charge, which unfortunately made headlines, was filed by Louisa on the grounds of mental cruelty, although she wanted to marry another man. Who knows? Uncle Booth had been a peripatetic, drinking *bon vivant.* She was very pretty, spoiled, and fond of masculine attention. And my grandmother, who never concealed her feelings, was probably very wicked to Louisa. As devoted as he was to Hautie, Uncle Booth had asked his sister's husband to stop her from standing up for him during this unhappy time. (This request must have meant that Nana really was using all her big guns.) The couple separated, getting a divorce late in 1911. Their daughter, Laurel, was left in the sole custody of her mother except for one month in the summer when she went to her father in Maine and visited him infrequently in Indianapolis.

My parents were sometimes in Kennebunkport when Laurel was there. My father said that she and her nurse used to stand on a little promontory and wave as the Tarkington boat, filled with guests, went out to sea for an afternoon of looking for whales. One would think that it would be a dream come true for Laurel to go on such an outing, but she never did. Maybe they thought she was too young, maybe she did not want to go, or maybe she was already showing some symptoms of the tragic illness that killed her. I never knew the answer.

Years later while we were in college, my cousin Mig and I used to visit the Tarkingtons in Maine. Once when we were exploring the woods behind the house, we came across an abandoned playhouse in a small clearing. We went in and found everything a child could desire — china tea sets, table and chairs, dolls, doll clothes on hangers, a stove — all diminutive. It had been built for Laurel. I forget what else was there, but I am sure nothing had been left out. It all looked so forlorn. I wonder whether she ever played in it. Were playmates imported to play with her? I do not know, but it is not much fun to play alone — even in a little dream house. My father has told me that Laurel seemed to him to be a lonely but very bright child, and she always arrived at Seawood, the Maine house, with a nurse.

◆ ◆ ◆ ◆ ◆ ◆ ◆ ◆ ◆

AFTER HIS DIVORCE AND BEFORE HIS SECOND MARRIAGE, Uncle Booth made additional trips abroad, often taking members of our family with him. My family has said, probably apocryphally, that Uncle Booth made and spent two fortunes during those trips and at home. Maybe it was true. He made most of his money before the income tax was levied. He was very extravagant and very generous when he was in Indianapolis, and easily the most popular man at the European nightspots because of the size of his tips. (He even tipped his *own chauffeur* for driving him someplace.)

My father has told me of a trip on which Uncle Booth took him when my father was a junior in Princeton. One evening just at dusk, Uncle Booth and my father entered the celebrated Parisian nightclub Maxim's. Uncle Booth had not been there for eight years. The owner was in the main room of the dimly lit club as they entered. He peered at them in the gloom, then rushed to Uncle Booth, kissed him on both cheeks, and shouted, "Allumez! Allumez! Monsieur Tarkington est ici!" Lights flooded the club and a wonderful party began. Uncle Booth offered a gold louis to the first chorus girl who could persuade my father to dance with her. (Later, as was Uncle

Booth's custom, each one of the chorus girls received a gold louis.) As a climax to the evening, he stood on a chair and taught all the patrons to sing a Princeton song that ended, "And to hell with Yale." Uncle Booth may have been traveling partly to heal marital wounds, but he succeeded in giving my father the most glorious time that he ever had.

My father told another story of an evening at the theater in Paris. He and Uncle Booth were in a box which was enclosed by heavy velvet curtains about twelve feet high, hung from brass poles. During the play they heard a sound from above and, looking up, beheld the genial equine face of George Arliss, the English character actor, peering benignly down upon them — seemingly disembodied. But my father was living in such a dream world that nothing would have surprised him. Arliss, in an adjoining box, had heard a familiar voice — Uncle Booth's — and had stood on his chair to look over the curtain. Nothing would do but they make a night of it. They arrived back at their hotel as the sun was rising. Uncle Booth, having bought an armload of violets from a flower vendor, presented them with a deep bow to the startled women who were scrubbing down the stone steps leading to the hotel lobby.

Some of their exploits during this trip abroad are lost in the mists of time or have been carefully edited. I suspect the latter. Uncle Booth told me once with a wicked smile that if I ever got into trouble with my father to ask him about the little Swiss girl in Geneva.

◆ ◆ ◆ ◆ ◆ ◆ ◆ ◆ ◆

IN 1911 WHILE HE WAS STILL MARRIED TO LOUISA, though separated, he met Susanah Keifer Robinson of Dayton, Ohio, where *The Man from Home* was then playing. Aunt Susanah told me, long after Uncle Booth's death, that they had met for the first time as dinner partners at a candlelit table, and I remember her saying to me, "There were just the two of us there in the candlelight." Although it was love at first sight, she forbade correspondence because he was still married. As soon as he was divorced, she permitted him to write to her; however, she turned down his proposal of marriage until he promised to stop drinking. He loved her enough to make a heroic and successful effort, and they were married in 1912. Although Uncle Booth never drank again, the Tarkingtons served liquor to their friends. Once during Prohibition,

Aunt Susanah timidly asked my father for the name of his bootlegger, saying, "Booth doesn't know about this, but I have to have sherry to serve to my friends."

Many, many years later, Uncle Booth and I were taking a walk, and I said to him, "I wonder what it's like to be an alcoholic." I did not know he had ever had a drinking problem. His answer was a brief sentence: "You're an alcoholic when you can't get out of bed in the morning without taking a drink first." I believe it was on the same walk I asked him how he knew when he was really through writing a book. The reply was equally succinct: "When I feel like vomiting if I look at it."

No reminiscences of Uncle Booth would be adequate without a description of Aunt Susanah, his truly beautiful second wife. The very adjectives seem hackneyed: short, a little plump, unwrinkled, with beautiful posture, direct grey eyes, exquisite in dress, and above all, gracious. She could have given lessons to sovereigns in queenliness, which to me means exquisite manners. One of her nieces said of her that as a young woman Aunt Susanah had "allure." I think she had allure all of her life. Certainly men, from two years to eighty-two, fell under her charm; and she was one of those women who invariably bring out the best in anyone. My husband and I used to take our daughters to see her when they were very small, an occasion fraught with possible disaster, but we need not have worried. They might have had tantrums when shoved into snowsuits at home, but they were all parents could dream of with Aunt Susanah. They, too, fell under her spell. In fact, my nephew, when he was four years old, asked her to marry him. She was completely feminine always, and she had one of the greatest of all gifts — one that men certainly admire and look for: she knew how to listen, and it was total listening.

"Susanah," she used to say to me with a smile, "sometimes I think that manners are almost more important than morals." Coming from a person whose own morals and manners were impeccable, this was indeed a strong statement, but it indicated a truth about Aunt Susanah. Underlying her charming and often regal manner was a shrewd, somewhat iconoclastic sense of humor.

I have often wondered how she made Hautie capitulate. It was not a role Nana was used to. I can only guess, but Aunt Susanah, in addition to the qualities I have mentioned, also had wisdom and patience. I am sure she was sweet and gracious to my grandmother and was unruffled by any barbs shot in her direction. If there was one fault that Aunt Susanah hated above all, it was complaining. She often spoke about it, and warned me never to do it. So, of course, she herself never would have complained to Uncle Booth about his older sister. So there were no three-way fights or tugs-of-war, with Uncle Booth in the middle. Nana, used to having her way with feminine in-laws, must have been outmaneuvered because Aunt Susanah never seemed upset or dismayed. If she were hurt, she kept her own counsel. A soft answer must really have turned away wrath.

I think that during his lifetime we enjoyed Uncle Booth more than we enjoyed Aunt Susanah, and this was as she chose it to be. She always made him the center of a group, the pivot of attention, a position which he graciously accepted. She never competed. She did not have to. But how many women could have resisted the temptation? He had lived with competitive females during much of his life, so he appreciated her rare quality. During the days following Uncle Booth's death, a nephew by marriage said to me, "I think that now we will begin really to appreciate Aunt Susanah."

♦ ♦ ♦ ♦ ♦ ♦ ♦ ♦ ♦

MY FATHER SAID ONCE, "WE HAVE SO MUCH FUN WITH Uncle Booth that we forget he's a famous man." And so we did. To me he was just Uncle Booth, and he was magic.

To understand even partially the aura that Uncle Booth projected to my generation, one needs some idea of the surroundings in which he lived and in which we knew him so well as we grew up in Indianapolis.

He, whose youthful devil-may-care antics in New York, Rome, Paris, and Capri were legend, had, by the time I knew him, settled into a serene and sheltered existence surrounded by the art objects he had collected in his wanderings. He went out only to see the family, visit the art museum, or hear the symphony. He told a reporter, "I began going to Maine forty-two years ago, but I always come back to Indiana. Your heart lies where home is."[20] Nowadays many people are rootless, returning to their birthplaces only for weddings or funerals, but Uncle Booth's roots lay deep in Indiana. How else could he have written so compellingly of the midlands? He revealed the depth of his roots when he wrote his nephews, "Your two G'fathers came to Indianapolis when there were only a few acres of shanties and boardwalks and mud, and Fall Creek ran through the Columbia Club and the legislature met in a woodshed."[21]

Donald   Laurel   Booth

Papa John   Trixie   John -   1913

Above: *In a 1913 photo, Laurel, Tarkington's daughter, is surrounded by
her grandfather Tarkington (Papa
John); (*left to right*) her cousins
Donald, Booth, and John; and a
family pet, Trixie.* Left: *John Jameson, Susanah Jameson Mayberry's
father and Hautie's eldest son, in
1911 when his uncle Booth took him
to Europe.*

Susanah Keifer Tarkington, the author's second wife, was called affectionately a "gentle dragon" because she guarded her husband from interruptions while he was writing. Above left: *In 1912, the year of her marriage to Tarkington.* Above right: *In a formal pose at about age forty-five.* Right: *At Seawood in her early seventies.*

When did I first truly remember him and his magic? It was Christmas night, 1929. My parents, my little brother Johnny, and I went to the Tarkingtons for a visit. There are those who consider childish memories unreliable, but this visit has such clarity that many later events seem dim by comparison. The Tarkington house at 4270 North Meridian Street stood far from the smoky center of town, and it was a muted fairyland to me. Outside was cold and black, but inside the house was warm and lovely. It is not often that a pinpoint in time and space can later be realized as a turning point — for all our moments are fluid — a compound of echoes from the past, the present moment, and wonderings about the future. But that Christmas night over fifty years ago marked my first conscious and specific recollections of Uncle Booth.

Wearing dinner clothes, he was sitting in a brown velvet chair by the fire. One of his specially-made Turkish cigarettes burned between very long and slightly shaking fingers. How impressed I was when I eventually discovered that his initials were on each cigarette. (Years afterwards I sneaked one of those cigarettes home, and one puff nearly did me in.) Later memories of Uncle Booth have added dimension to that evening's memories of him, but what remains with me clearly are brown eyes twinkling behind heavy glasses and a haze of cigarette smoke.

His voice? At that tender age I could not have described it, but time has helped me articulate what I heard. It was resonant, had a deep timbre, and, though soft, carried when he spoke. I still do not know what makes a quiet voice more noticeable than a loud one. In his case, maybe it was a feeling that *this* voice had something special to say and that its owner had a more vivid presence than others in the room. At Princeton Uncle Booth had been a soloist in the glee club, and no evening of beer and singing was complete until Tark stood on a table and rendered "Danny Deever." He made this song famous at Princeton many years before I was born, but the baritone resonance lingered in his speaking voice throughout his life.

To me he seemed old. But then my parents seemed old, and they were no doubt in their early thirties. As a child of eight, I would not have used the word *electric,* but I recognized even then that he had a voltage that made the other people in the room seem dim. I remember feeling expectant. He was playing with a large pair of dice which he had received for Christmas, and I wondered why.

Before settling down beside him, Johnny and I made our tour, looking at our favorite treasures (so we must have been in the house before). We thought they were our *own* special treasures. Only much later did I realize that some of them were priceless, collected during Uncle Booth's visits to Europe — living evidence of his quintessential discrimination and taste. In the sunroom we trailed our fingers in the shallow water of the Greek white marble trough which always held long-stemmed pink roses, noticing casually in passing the marble French Gothic madonnas who smiled eternally at their happy babies. We looked longingly at the golden Spanish desk, taller than a man, intricately carved, and containing, we were sure, many secret drawers; but parental nervousness had communicated itself, and we were loath to explore it. Much later, in 1944, this desk became an altar, banked by palms and candles; and my husband and I were married in front of it while Uncle Booth smiled at us, half hidden from us by the palms, and wholly hidden from the wedding guests.

That Christmas night I noticed, not his treasured portraits themselves — except for the pleasure in the glint of a sword hilt or a jewel — but the lights which illuminated them. Each painting had its own light with a shade attached to the top of the frame. How odd this seemed to me. In our house, lights were on tables or in the ceilings. Much later when we were more educable, Uncle Booth used to explain the portraits and the painters. He once said that most of them in his Indianapolis house were of fifteenth- or sixteenth-century men and women and added, "They were a hard people because they had to be. Most of them look capable of murder and that is because they were." This, of course, delighted us.

My own favorite treasure in the house was the carved wooden head of a young Greek boy with curly hair, his eyes gazing serenely into middle distance. I loved the feel of him. His ancient sculptor was asking that he be caressed, and I always did just that. My brother's favorite was what we always called "the poison ring." It was big enough for a giant and had probably been used to seal Renaissance correspondence; but since it opened at one end where one just might put poison in it, we chose, of course, to believe it had been used lethally. Uncle Booth never said anything to dissuade us.

He had his own favorite "treasure," which he loved to tell us about, and I think he did that evening. I believe that no purchase of an antique ever gave him more pleasure than the acquisition of his marble faun. Uncle Booth described him in *Your Amiable Uncle:*

> *He stood six-feet-two on his pedestal of mottled green*
> *marble, cut from a column that Hadrian ravished from Egypt*
> *and that sank in the Tiber with a shipload which Alaric the Goth*
> *was bearing away after he sacked Rome. . . . He really belonged*

to me.... No antique comes near him to my mind and heart....
My fellow is so real ... and so lazy and so understandful. How
he must have laughed in his sleepy way at the girls who
followed him and posed at him. He is not a gentleman at all ...
he is just a clever, idle, pure, winesipping, chestnut-eating, faun
... dreamland humorist in marble.[22]

Now the same faun stands, still smiling lazily, in a specially
made niche at my brother's house. Depending on the season, his
children have added autumn leaves or holly wreaths to his vine
leaves. I have seen him bedecked with a wreath of chrysanthemums
or, even, a fedora.

That evening I remember wondering why the Tarkingtons did
not put their Christmas cards on the mantel as we did. They were in
a decorated basket on the hearth. Much later I sensed that it would
have been a desecration to put anything so trivial on that gorgeous
piece of stone, carved after one that Francis I had at the Cluny
Palace.

One of Uncle Booth's greatest traits was that he *never* disappointed children. Many parents must plead guilty to this charge, but
not he. After our tour of treasures, we settled down beside him. He
gave us the dice he had been holding, told us how to take turns, and
said, "I'll give five dollars to the first child who throws a seven." I, at
least, was struck dumb. (The most money I had ever had was an
occasional dime from the tooth fairy.) And I won! Five whole dollars
just for me. My little brother's disappointment meant absolutely
nothing to me. Then, Uncle Booth said, "I'll give five dollars to the
first boy who throws a seven." I was ecstatic. Maybe five more
dollars just for me. In my avarice I had not even heard the word *boy.*
Anyway, after the game — and I have never since played one like
it — both Johnny and I went home with ten dollars apiece, and
neither of us has ever forgotten how very rich we were. The feeble
talk of parents about putting the money into our savings-and-loan
accounts went unheeded. This money of ours was to be hoarded and
gloated over. Magic, indeed. That is the only word for that Christmas
night.

◆ ◆ ◆ ◆ ◆ ◆ ◆ ◆ ◆

OUR FALLING UNDER UNCLE BOOTH'S SPELL THAT NIGHT
so long ago may have been intensified by natural childish acquisitiveness, but the spell went on during our childhood and young

adulthood. Memories of other evenings in his Indianapolis house and in Seawood form a kaleidescope: Uncle Booth smiling behind his cigarette smoke; Betty Trotter, his secretary, bending over a manuscript as she read it aloud to us; Aunt Susanah sitting serenely by the fire, inexpertly knitting (my mother always had to turn the heels of the bed socks which she made for every family member); Figaro, the poodle, his garnet eyes gleaming in the firelight. The very lights and shadows seemed pink tinted, but maybe memory makes me hallucinate. More likely, the silk lampshades were a warm color.

We were in our generation six great-nieces and great-nephews who grew up having the time of our lives during these visits. These nieces and nephews, now past middle age, are the children of the nephews who provided copy for the Penrod stories. We were just ordinary everyday children. We had our own lives, fairly happy, I guess, and uneventful except for the usual childhood crises, but we had what *only* six children have ever had: Uncle Booth. Our frequent visits with him, when he was in Indianapolis, provided a kind of exclamation point to our lives. We accepted his magic as children accept most gifts — without questioning. His comings and goings and his distinguished guests made the front page. But for us, he was mainly the head of the family, and our family's cohesion was increased by his interest in us and his love for all of us. Did we make the most of our wonderful opportunity? Maybe not, but we certainly had fun. As I reminisce I wonder what is the most important thing one person can offer another. Do you think it might be enjoyment?

When I attempt to describe the host who presided benignly over all this fun, words seem pale. My memory is vivid, though *memory* is hardly the right word. It is more as if I have been carrying Uncle Booth in my mind and heart for many years. He always seemed in top form during our visits. He had a *joie de vivre,* a perfect graciousness, and an innate ability to make old people feel younger, young people feel older, and everyone feel involved and alive.

His appearance? My actual memories of him span about twenty years, so the later ones seem more vivid. He laughed often — and always silently. His long mobile face almost always reflected amusement — that is, unless he were discussing FDR, or a Picasso he hated which the Herron Museum of Art in Indianapolis had bought over his veto, or when he was exposed to a crashing bore for longer than he thought was humane. Much of his amused expression must have been because he was laughing at us, although we did not realize it and would not have cared if we had known.

He was very masculine though frail and, at least in his later years, a little stooped. He had a prominent nose (a Tarkington feature) and a comedian's wide mouth, and above all, he was distinguished looking. Brown eyes spoke and twinkled behind heavy glasses, and there was always one of his ever present Turkish cigarettes held in slightly shaking long fingers.

In dress he was elegant and fastidious and in his earlier days might have been called "a dandy." Long ago a contemporary of his, after a Seawood visit, came home saying, "Tark's got peach-colored pants." And this was long before men wore colors. The Tarkington family dressed for dinner, and I will always remember his black patent leather evening slippers with flat grosgrain bows on the front. It seems funny to me now that I never thought this foot attire the least bit unusual. The slippers seemed perfectly appropriate. When my husband returned from World War II, the first article of civilian clothing he received was from Uncle Booth. It was a heavy, beautiful blue-and-gray tweed jacket which his friend Kenneth Roberts had given him. Uncle Booth handed it to Frank, with a chuckle, saying, "It makes me look too authorish."

A natural magnetism surrounded his person. Without doing anything or saying a word, he became the center of attention though he never exhibited any consciousness of fame or importance. But this magnetism came about as often as not through his habit of being an absorbed listener. He was a dazzlingly entertaining conversationalist, and he had a store of fascinating, often hilarious anecdotes about nearly every theatrical and literary celebrity of his day; but when *you* talked to him, he listened as though what you were saying was the most absorbing thing he had ever heard. This was a not inconsiderable part of his great charm.

In most households when children are told that a visit to a person they consider "old" is in the offing, the reaction is predictable and always negative. Not so with us. We looked forward to our visits to Uncle Booth with the keenest anticipation. Can you imagine the different generations in a family really enjoying each other? One of Nature's immutable laws, it seems to me, is that at mixed-generation groups the children have fun or the grown-ups have fun, but rarely both. But at the Tarkingtons, everybody had fun. Not mild enjoyment, but sidesplitting hilarity was usually part of these evenings.

When we were with Uncle Booth, the bar that separates the generations disappeared entirely, and we discovered each other. I think part of the true gayety — alas, now so scarce — was that we were stimulated by his delighted enjoyment of us. There are those rare people who bring out the best in you, and rarer still are those who do it without your realizing it because you are having too much fun. My memories of those evenings are that we were all smarter, gayer, and happier than at any other time.

Uncle Booth thought that adults did not often find children irresistible — except their own, and then only sometimes. He wrote that he, himself, had forfeited the "love and admiration" of grown-up people "by the simple process of growing."[23] This seems to me almost indisputable for all children, and I can only say that with Uncle Booth we did not forfeit it. His constant interest in children and his curiosity about the psychology of youth was, of course, legend by the time we knew him, although we did not realize it when we were young. He knew very well that children consider adults as the opposition. His delight was to find out, if we did, why we did. If a warning glance went from child to parent or parent to child, he always intercepted it, no matter how veiled it was, and interpreted it perfectly. Undercurrents delighted him, and if he suspected trouble brewing, his joy was unconcealed. He was probably sympathetic to harassed parents, but we never knew it.

◆ ◆ ◆ ◆ ◆ ◆ ◆ ◆ ◆

IF THE NEPHEWS WHOSE DELINQUENCIES HAD INSPIRED *Penrod* had forgotten to mention them to their children, he saw to it that we were kept informed. Naturally we received those biographical illuminations with pure rapture. There is nothing more satisfying, if you are in trouble over a report card, than to be told that when your father was your age he was in trouble with the police. Not only had our fathers been young once, they had been juvenile delinquents of considerable stature.

We closely watched our fathers during these stories, waiting hopefully for them to show embarrassment or shame. Not at all. They laughed until they cried and interrupted each other in their eagerness to add yet another more horrible story of youthful crime. They seemed proud of having derailed streetcars! Uncle Booth's favorite story was about a summer when my father and uncle tapped into a telephone line behind the barn of the family home at Eleventh and Pennsylvania. They then ordered two quarts of ice cream to be delivered daily to the porch of a neighbor who was out of town and charged to him. They stole the ice cream and went behind the barn to gorge themselves as they talked long distance to their friends in Maxinkuckee, Indiana.

There was one story that Uncle Booth told, which, for me, was the most memorable of all, probably because I wondered what would have happened to *me* if I had done it. This occurred when my father and my uncle were children. Impressed or maddened by the decor of a newly decorated room in their house called "the Turkish room," they had wheeled in enough wheelbarrows of sand from a building site next door to completely cover the floor of the room. And this on a day when their mother was about to have one of her famous and probably dreaded salons to entertain visiting celebrities. Uncle Booth's theatrical and literary friends, when they were in Indianapolis, were coerced into being "lions" at Hautie's tea parties. They usually acquiesced because of their fondness for him.

Oh, those soirées. I am still, some fifty years later, covered with shame over my behavior at one of them. I had been invited to my grandmother's, at my request, to meet Miss Helen Hayes. She was in Indianapolis then, playing in *Mary, Queen of Scots.* I had seen the play and she had become my instant idol. On my way to the tea party my mind was full of witticisms with which I would entertain her and of the fears that I might disgrace myself. At the party we sat side by side on a horsehair sofa. She turned to me and said kindly, "And are you interested in the theater?" So much for my plans for repartee. I was so paralyzed with embarrassment that I could hardly speak. Thickly, I muttered one word: "No." She turned to someone else and said that the Marrott Hotel had such nice percale sheets that she need not have packed her own. I was so mortified that I said not one more word and very soon escaped in shame.

One day, according to my father who was an unwilling guest, Uncle Booth delightedly destroyed Nana's aplomb during an, oh, so genteel tea party. (Booth and Hautie's father was one of six children, and most of the offspring of those six were farmers or workmen.) Uncle Booth appeared at his sister's front door with a man in stained work clothes, saying, "Here's Cousin Jim Tarkington. He's working out in front on the streetcar tracks, and I've invited him to the party." It was not easy to nonplus Nana, but her brother knew how (as do most siblings). Cousin Jim mingled courteously among the guests, balancing a teacup and cucumber sandwiches. If looks could have killed, a literary career would have probably ended that afternoon. Cousin Jim departed with the other guests and went back to work on the streetcar tracks. I imagine that his Cousin Booth escaped as soon as possible.

As I have said, Uncle Booth dearly loved to reveal our father's youthful exploits. One night he told us, always an eager audience, that years before when my father was a little boy, Uncle Booth had something very private to discuss with his sister, my father's mother. As he began the conversation, he said he knew absolutely that my father was hiding in the room listening, though he had heard no rustle nor any movement that would betray the eavesdropper. Before beginning the confidential part of the conversation, he said to my grandmother, "Hautie, I have to tell you something about John. He bit Katie Johnson twice during recess today." He found out what he was after. The answer to his statement was an enraged denial from the hidden boy: "I did not! I did not!"

We did not always have these biographical highlights for entertainment. Sometimes we played a game and often Betty Trotter, Uncle Booth's secretary, would read to us the latest *Rumbin Gallery* or *Ripley Little* story. Or we might be greatly entertained by Uncle Booth's conversation and storytelling. He could find a good story in anything that had the slightest significance, and he was a storyteller par excellence.

He was, in addition, a gifted mimic in many languages. So we rejoiced in his dialect stories. I found out later that he used to amuse himself by calling my father or uncle on the telephone at their office and in broken dialect embark on a frightful and highly colored hardluck story, the upshot of which was that he could not possibly make his payments. As well as they knew his ordinary speaking voice, his dialect always fooled them because he varied it each time. He never admitted making such calls. His aim was to enrage his nephews, and he usually succeeded, at least with my father. To my recollection Uncle Booth used the telephone only for these calls and when he called my parents on December 7, 1941, to tell them the Japanese had bombed Pearl Harbor.

As I have said, he once took his brother-in-law and my father for a memorable trip abroad in 1911. I well remember my father telling me that once during the Paris stay my grandfather was taking the air in a dignified and straight-backed way, when Uncle Booth, dressed as a Paris pimp, crept up to him and whined in low-life Parisian dialect that he could get him a "nice plump boy." The act was an obvious success because my grandfather began to cane him.

Uncle Booth as writer was probably in an enviable position during those evenings his grandnieces and grandnephews spent with him. We were invited, encouraged, egged on by him, probably analyzed more than a bit, and then our parents took us home before he could get too tired. I feel sure now that we did provide firsthand

Right: *A formal photographic portrait shows Tarkington with an ever-present cigarette held between his fingers.* Below: *In 1937 at seventy-five, Hautie Tarkington Jameson entertains her son Booth in the grand manner reminiscent of the days when she entertained theatrical and literary friends of her brother Booth.*

Above left to right: *Johnny, Susie, and "the Divine Flora" Jameson, the great-nephew and great-nieces, whose lives were touched by the* magic of their amiable uncle. Below: *In the alcove of the room pictured, "the Divine Flora" resisted being christened.*

copy, but we did not know it then. However, anyone who has read Tarkington's novels about childhood knows that his literary creations were not mysterious children — no Tinker Bells or Peter Pans — but flesh-and-blood children suffering the trials usual to growing up. No wonder if he set the stage a bit and did some egging on. We, in a sense, took Penrod's place. My uncle had the first prerequisite for anyone who writes truly about human nature: curiosity. Overriding even that was his great love for his family. He had long since turned his back on gayer and wilder times, and he may partially have substituted observation of us as one of his diversions and, too, as grist for his mill.

We always went home reluctantly, shivering in the cold after the warmth of the fire and wondering why the magic did not last. I remember saying to my brother after one of those evenings, "Our house is dumb compared to the Tarkingtons'." After one of our visits to Uncle Booth, our own surroundings seemed pallid and, most of all, unexciting. And when could we go to see him again?

Even as children we knew, but could not express, what Julian Street later did in a eulogy at the time of Uncle Booth's death:

> There was a kind of magic about Mr. Tarkington . . . I have
> often tried to analyze it, but how can magic be analyzed? How
> can one say what makes a room change when a certain person
> comes into it, or what makes all attention wait upon that
> person? Mr. Tarkington's magic seemed to be compounded of
> great intelligence, great acuteness or perception and an
> extraordinary sense of humor that held his other qualities in
> perfect balance. Fastidiousness governed all the departments of
> Mr. Tarkington's life. In person, dress, language and thought he
> was immaculate.[24]

To this I would like to add his manners. Though he never suffered fools or incompetents gladly, he always did it with courtesy, at least when he was with them. I remember his telling us once that he had been interviewed by an eager young reporter who said to him, "Now I'd like an informal picture of you taken in the kitchen opening a bottle of beer." With perfect politeness, I am sure, he had replied, "I haven't had a bottle of beer for thirty years, and I've *never* been in the kitchen." He was correct on both counts.

Once he just could not resist telling us about a lady, a well-born southern lady, who had been his dinner partner. She had thrust an expensively and exquisitely shod foot at him and said in fluting southern accents, "I just can't wear factory-made shoes. I have to have my shoes made by hand to fit my little Virginia foot." He quoted her verbatim, but instead of her cultured southern accent, known to us all, he used a honeyed southern drawl.

♦ ♦ ♦ ♦ ♦ ♦ ♦ ♦ ♦

I MENTIONED THAT THE HERRON MUSEUM OF ART purchased a Picasso painting over Uncle Booth's vociferous objections. At that time both he and his good friend and contemporary Caroline Fesler were members of the museum's fine arts committee, the body that voted for additions to the museum's collection. She was in favor of the Picasso. The bond between the two friends, who greatly respected and admired one another, was strengthened as a result of their heated and repeated arguments about Picasso. She was extremely interested in some of the modern art of the first half of the twentieth century, while he as always was drawn to the traditional, the representational. In addition to this, he felt somehow betrayed by Picasso, believing that he was a painter of genius who had begun to prostitute his art. In any case Uncle Booth and Mrs. Fesler remained devoted friends.

It was her pleasure to invite musical virtuosi of the day to play for her. When she invited a musician to play at her home, the guest list was limited, but the Tarkingtons were always present. Once in the thirties when Walter Gieseking, the world-famous German-born pianist, was playing for her, Uncle Booth sat very close to the piano. The two men had never met before, but a strong percipience, an inexplicable link occurred between them. Minds did not need to meet; hearts and spirits were the common bond. Speech was superfluous; eyes and a brief handshake conveyed the feeling. Uncle Booth knew absolutely that they both felt this bond, and he was very moved when he spoke about it. If he could not define it, I certainly cannot. "There are more things in heaven and earth, Horatio, than are dreampt of in your philosophy." Uncle Booth's almost spiritual connection with Gieseking obviously meant a great deal to him and he never forgot the moment. He mentioned it to me several times during the latter years of his life. It did not seem to matter to him whether Gieseking had forgotten the incident or not. The importance was that it had occurred.

♦ ♦ ♦ ♦ ♦ ♦ ♦ ♦ ♦

UNCLE BOOTH ONCE WROTE CONCERNING HIS BOYHOOD that when a grown-up's "gaze guardedly fell upon me, it expressed consciousness of being in the presence of something chancy and likely to be objectionable."[25] Any situation involving anxious adults and mutinous children turned him into a delighted conspirator hoping the children *would be* "objectionable" and doing his best to make sure that they were. In our family annals, just such an occasion is recorded when I was twelve. It was the christening of my little sister, Florence, who was five. The room at my grandmother's house where the event was to occur was filled with our large family — adults on one side of the room and about twelve restless, dressed-up children who were inexpressibly bored on the other. Strategically speaking, the arrangement was unfortunate. Uncle Booth stood in the doorway looking as if he were enjoying himself. A few adults eyed him warily. The christenée, who stood in front of the minister and was firmly held by the hands of her parents, kept muttering, "I don't wanna be christened. Johnny told me it would hurt." She had dug in her heels and locked her knees and pulled herself as far from the minister as possible. The minister was an old man — or so *we* thought — and he read the baptism service in the high sweet monotone of the almost totally deaf.

We children were milling restlessly, giggling, poking each other, and in general looking for trouble. Our collective fuse was very short. As the minister droned, "Dost thou renounce the devil and all his works, the vain pomp and glory of the world . . . ," suddenly from the children's side came the sound of music accompanied by titters. My little brother had sat on the antique musical chair, and the strains of *Marche Militaire* tinkled loudly through the room. Uncle Booth leaned forward shaking with laughter as we pushed and pinched to get a chance to sit on the chair. More droning. "In the unity of the Holy Spirit be all honor and glory. . . ." A look of unholy joy came into Uncle Booth's face. Pulling out of his pockets two handfuls of coins, he sent them spinning into the midst of the children, then backed quickly out of the doorway. Pandemonium. My sister, forgetting her own problems, wrenched away from her parents' grasp and dived across the room into the melee of crawling children. Her body position was like that of a child doing a belly flop into the water — back arching and arms and legs flailing. She yelled above the tumult, "Gimme some! Gimme some!"

The minister, holding a silver bowl filled with real holy water from the River Jordan (my grandmother had boiled it, fearing germs), looked around in a sweet and puzzled way. The racket had evidently escaped him. Florence extricated herself from the mass of children and marched back to the minister. Dress torn, hair ribbon untied, firmly holding two fistfuls of coins, she leaned forward to receive the holy water and minister's blessing.

At the refreshment party that followed, the donor of the largesse was nowhere in sight.

◆ ◆ ◆ ◆ ◆ ◆ ◆ ◆ ◆

IN 1921 UNCLE BOOTH WAS AT THE HEIGHT OF HIS fame and Princeton, DePauw, and Columbia managed to give him degrees before he began to refuse invitations to appear at commencements. Purdue, though, arranged to give him one by holding an academic procession in his own house in 1940.

My younger sister was then eleven and I was away at college. I have asked her what she remembers most about that day: (1) she got to stay out of school; (2) it was a beautiful warm spring day; (3) she was very, very impressed by the brilliant academic hoods; (4) the procession marched through the wide front yard and onto an open porch in front of the house; and (5) she recalls wondering why such a fuss was being made over Uncle Booth and that he had a funny "hat" on.

The *Indianapolis Star* had more to say:

> *Purdue University set aside academic tradition yesterday and moved more than a score of deans and dignitaries off the campus to the Booth Tarkington residence here to add a new honor to the myriad possessed by the world-renowned Indiana novelist. In the living room of the Tarkington home . . . President Edward C. Elliott conferred upon the author the honorary degree of doctor of humane letters. . . .*
>
> *Mr. Tarkington, whose health has been none too good all winter long, was not able to make a trip to Lafayette, so the University came to him instead. Deeply moved by the recognition he said nothing but "thank you" when the degree was conferred.*
>
> *James W. Noel, Indianapolis attorney and member of the Purdue Board of Trustees, presented the degree and said in part: "From the* Gentleman from Indiana *to the* Rumbin Galleries, *he has run the entire gamut of American life, ennobling youth and stimulating ambition, ridiculing pretence and satirizing hypocrisy. For fine humor he has taken rank with Mark Twain. . . .*

Purdue's policy for many years was to award honorary
degrees to those who have been students, faculty or staff members
there. Mr. Tarkington, who did most of his college work at
Princeton, was on the West Lafayette campus in 1890 – 1891 and
appears on the records as "Newton B. Tarkington. . . ." The citation
presented to the author was designed by Bruce Rogers eminent
American typologist, also a student at Purdue in 1890. . . .[26]

He began to win popularity contests which he thought silly, but
he was pleased in 1933 to receive the gold medal previously
awarded to William Dean Howells and Edith Wharton by the
National Institute of Arts and Letters and in 1945 to be given the
William Dean Howells medal, awarded only once in five years from
the American Academy of Arts and Letters. Aunt Susanah went to
New York to accept it for him as he could not make the trip.

Sinclair Lewis, author of the citation speech, wrote, " 'Mr.
Tarkington . . . has been one of the first and he remains one of the
chiefs of all the discoverers of America in literature. . . . Perhaps as
much as Hamlin Garland or Howells or Dreiser he was a pioneer in
seeing that our wheatfields and apple trees and old brownstone-
fronts are quite as romantic as European marble fauns and secret
gardens.' "[27]

As well as doing his own prodigious work, Uncle Booth always
found time to encourage struggling writers. The following is some
advice which I use because it is so true of his own writing. He told
young authors that the characters, not the author, made the plot,
adding that " 'It is unusual poignancy that makes a book unusual,
not unusual plot.' " He said to pick " 'your reader: the best reader
you have inside *you* . . . then play with his imagination. Startle him,
amuse him, make him see what *you* see — make him feel your
words — flush him with colors.' " And most importantly " *'always* by
suggestion. Make *him* tell the story.' " His advice was to " 'use closed
doors . . . Suggest — give him a smell, that's all.' " He thought, too,
that the used word was stale and told the writer he must get " 'living
words out of himself.' "[28]

Julian Street's words about Uncle Booth's writing echo and
emphasize my uncle's own advice to young authors:

He insisted on the right of characters in fiction or the drama to
decent privacy. Embraces were never described in his stories or
seen in his plays. The lovers might be moving toward each other
as the chapter ended or the curtain fell, but that was all. His
feeling was . . . that a love scene skillfully foreshadowed was far
more beautiful in the imagination of an audience than printed
words or visible acts could make it.[29]

And Uncle Booth wrote scenes as he advised they should be written. In the conclusion of one of his early books, *The Conquest of Canaan,* the hero and heroine sit together in church. They have just realized that each loves the other. The young woman has taken off her gloves, and the man is holding them reverently and looking down at them. ". . . something forlorn in his careful tenderness toward her so touched her that she felt the tears coming to her eyes with a sudden rush. And to prevent them, 'Not the empty gloves, Joe,' she whispered."[30]

◆ ◆ ◆ ◆ ◆ ◆ ◆ ◆ ◆

IN 1915 WHILE IN THE EAST, THE TARKINGTONS SAW Alfred Lunt play a small part in Uncle Booth's *The Country Cousin.* Delighted with Lunt's acting, my uncle went backstage to see him and invited the astonished young man to come to luncheon if he were ever in Indianapolis. Subsequently, Lunt came for Sunday dinner when he was on tour.

After dinner the two men retired to Uncle Booth's third-floor study. When a couple of hours had passed, Aunt Susanah went to the foot of the stairs to call them. The actor exploded out of the door, slid down the bannister sidesaddle, and whirled her around and around shouting, "I'm made! I'm made! He's going to write a play for me." The play was *Clarence,* a major triumph of Uncle Booth's playwriting career. With his own special talent, as was his custom, he had found an actor and shaped him into a character in a comic play.

On February 13, 1919, my uncle wrote to his producer about the feminine lead as follows:

> And, *if this play is played* got *to have Helen Hayes for the 16 to 18 year-old sister of the 16 to 18 year-old boy:* Got *to! This is the best girl or woman part I ever managed to write . . . and needs just that one young genius-person H. H. to play it. . . .*

And on February 25 he described his use of Alfred Lunt's handsomeness:

> You'll see I've made use of Lunt's extraordinary good looks, by leading UP to them: disguising them for a time – partly at least. I believe he has the full limit of "manly beauty": my idea was to take full comedy value of this endowment and not sell it for a nickel at first sight.[31]

Uncle Booth's remarks about Alfred Lunt's appearance may need some explanation for anyone who has not seen or read *Clarence* or who has never seen Lunt. When Lunt, who, of course, was Clarence, first appeared on stage, he was certainly not a prepossessing figure. His posture was terrible, he shambled, talked jerkily and nervously, and wore a World War I uniform that was much too small for him. His wrists stuck out below the sleeves, and he turned the rim of his Army hat as he waited. There was not a hint of the stunning man that Alfred Lunt really was. Even at the end of the play, he, himself, seemed to play down his good looks because Clarence is such a self-effacing figure.

Critics and audiences alike were delighted with *Clarence,* and on opening night a standing audience demanded many curtain calls. The play was the beginning of a lifelong friendship between Uncle Booth and Lunt and was an impetus to the career of Miss Hayes. Uncle Booth thought it had that rare ingredient, a perfect cast, and insisted that the praises go to the actors.

In 1964, eighteen years after Uncle Booth's death, Lunt and his wife, Lynn Fontanne, visited Aunt Susanah for the celebration of the fiftieth anniversary of the Booth Tarkington Civic Theater in Indianapolis. Although no longer young, the actor and his wife had made a long and arduous trip to grace this occasion. *Clarence* was being performed, by amateurs of course, and it was extremely well done; the players were very conscious of Lunt's being in the audience.

I had never before seen the Lunts off stage, and they were extraordinarily beautiful — somehow larger than life. One only had to glance at them to know what superb human beings they were. A kind of aura surrounded both of them. And, of course, they played to the hilt on that occasion because of their real love for Aunt Susanah.

After the last curtain, the first Clarence took the stage. He was easily one of the most distinguished men I have ever seen — erect and dignified. His great charm reached us over the footlights. Every inch an actor, he complimented the performers and then gave a brief talk. He walked slowly back and forth, hands in his pockets, as at ease on stage as if he had been in his own living room. Looking at Aunt Susanah all the time, he related in an understated manner how he had received his start in the theater, telling the audience about that long-ago day when he joyously slid down the bannister at the Tarkingtons' shouting, "I'm made! I'm made!" He recreated the incident so vividly it was as if we had been there. He ended by telling us about the luck *Clarence* had brought him: he met Lynn Fontanne while it was running.

Lynn Fontanne was regal in a black velvet dress with a train. Of course, she was perfectly made up and had the presence possessed only by the really great theatrical performers. When introduced, she stood and bowed — as did Aunt Susanah upon her own introduction. Aunt Susanah's cheeks were pink from excitement (all her life she looked radiant when Uncle Booth was praised), and she was even more queenly than Miss Fontanne, though almost a head shorter. My aunt wore black lace and her hands and throat and hair twinkled with diamonds. Her lovely white hair was piled high on her head and she wore a tiny diamond tiara.

The evening was a smashing success for everyone except my unfortunate husband. He had not wanted to go in the first place because his two upper-front teeth were temporarily missing and he was afraid of being conspicuous. But this was a command performance. Of course, he was introduced to Miss Fontanne by Aunt Susanah. He was putting his coat on at the time. His right arm was halfway into the arm of his overcoat, and because of a torn lining, it got stuck right there. He could not get his arm all the way in or all the way out. The great lady of the theater graciously extended her hand to him, but he could not do a thing about it; and he dared not smile at her due to the gap in the front of his mouth. His struggles seemed interminable, and I stifled a giggle, earning a look of reproof from Aunt Susanah. She felt, of course, and was absolutely right, that this was not the appropriate time for levity. They never did shake hands. When Miss Fontanne extended her left hand, Frank gave it a feeble squeeze, mumbled something unintelligible, and fled, his arm still stuck and his coat dragging on the floor.

◆ ◆ ◆ ◆ ◆ ◆ ◆ ◆ ◆

FOR SEVERAL REASONS I AM DEVOTING SOME WORDS TO *Penrod,* published in 1913 — mainly, because it is so funny, but also, because if one thinks of Uncle Booth's books today, *Penrod,* if nothing else, comes to mind. (Once I asked Uncle Booth how he thought up the names of his characters. He told me he nearly always got them out of the telephone book. Bushrod Browning, he said, was the name he first gave to Penrod Schofield, but he changed it before publication.) *Penrod* also has special interest for me because my father and uncles were its models, as was the author himself. He told me that he could write a *Penrod* chapter in one sitting and that this

Because their mother, Hautie, insisted that they dress in finery, Tarkington's nephews were teased relentlessly by their peers and re-taliated by becoming the neighbor-hood terrors. Above left and right: *Donald and John in 1894.* Above right: *John, the father of this book's author, when he was eight.* Right left and right: *Again Donald and John at ten and twelve respectively.*

was the easiest writing he had ever done. He most certainly had a wealth of material from which to work. (Royalties still come in from *Penrod* sales, though I believe most of his other books are out of print.)

It is rare for a creator of adult fiction to write so humorously about a boy. Once when reading a new chapter to family members, Uncle Booth began to laugh so hard that Aunt Susanah chided him for undue merriment. He gasped, "I'm not laughing at what I've written. I'm laughing at how funny boys are."

Since Penrod and his alter ego, Sam Williams, played in the alley and stable, young people have become a national market, catered to by billion-dollar industries, specialized publications, and beleaguered parents and teachers. Perhaps the present cult of nostalgia, in which I partake, is an expression of a collective innocence we once knew that is now missing. Certainly young people can and do face serious, even terrifying problems — and many, many more of them today than in 1913 — but Penrod remains for us steadfastly lighthearted and uncomplicated.

Uncle Booth knew that certain deep desires are common to all boys. One is to be omnipotent in the world they so briefly inhabit; another, to be invisible to grown-ups. Penrod is continually on a collision course with the adult world. He takes himself extremely seriously, and thus the author creates comedy. Lying is, of course, one of Penrod's perennial defenses. To get himself out of trouble, Penrod piles lie upon lie to convince his teacher that his uncle is drunken and abusive, and she believes him. From experience Uncle Booth wrote: "Besides there are two things that will be believed of any man whatsoever and one of them is that he has taken to drink."[32]

Dancing class heads Penrod's list of horrors, and when the teacher announces a party, his gloom deepens. His partner, Marjorie Rennsdale, is his eleventh choice, a foot shorter, and several years younger than he. In addition, they cordially hate each other. On the afternoon of the dancing party, a deep depression fills his soul, not alleviated by the sight of his first choice, dressed in pink and carrying a sheaf of American Beauty roses, spinning by in a car with the young gentleman who is her escort. He sees them from the roof of the stable where he has his elbows crooked over the ridgepole. At the sight of the joyful pair, Penrod waves both hands to them, or "it may have been a gesture of despair. . . . Undeniably there must remain a suspicion of deliberate purpose."[33] He suddenly disappears from view.

At the beginning of the party, flushing with sudden relief, Miss Rennsdale curtsies to Professor Bartet and hands him a note addressed to herself:

Dear Madam

    Please excuse me from dancing the cotilon with you this afternoon as I have fell off the barn.

Sincerly yours

PENROD SCHOFIELD[34]

Except for the signature, this is the same letter Uncle Booth once wrote — even to the spelling.

Uncle Booth's terse summary put the exclamation point on the comedy which occurred when Penrod's zeal overextends itself. To be permitted to act in a play that Penrod and Sam give in the stable, Roderick Magsworth Bitts, a boy in the neighborhood, is forced to acknowledge kinship with an alleged murderess of the same middle name whose trial is making newspaper headlines. Roderick becomes Exhibit A, and a poster announcing the family connection is prominently displayed on the main street. When Roderick's mother, a self-important woman who takes family connections very seriously, discovers her son's part in the show, she appears in the stable loft breathing fire. The terrified Penrod even thinks he sees lightning playing around her head. Uncle Booth inimitably reduced the scene to two sentences. "There ensued a period when only a shrill keening marked the passing of Roderick as he was borne to the tumbril. Then all was silence."[35]

Uncle Booth in this book penetrated into a boy's world where morality is based on what you can get away with and imagination is more important than fact. Always interested in reactions, he revealed his knowledge of boy psychology: the more closely volcanoes, western rivers, nitroglycerin, and boys are pent, the deadlier is their reaction at the point of outbreak.

The stories were an instant success when they appeared serially in 1915 in *Everybody's Magazine,* and Uncle Booth received $5,500 for each chapter. They were published later in book form and translated into almost every major language. My brother-in-law, Dr. Mark Kac, a distinguished Polish-born mathematician, was enchanted when he learned that my uncle had written *Penrod.* He had read it and loved it when he was a boy in Poland. So Uncle Booth wrote a book loved by both adults and boys. The plethora of boy stories on the radio, in books, and on television owe a great deal to *Penrod.*

The atmosphere of these books is that of ineffable brightness and sunshine without shadows where life is a succession of todays. I think Uncle Booth's uncanny acuteness about people is in part the reason for *Penrod*'s longevity. Unlike many men, he never forgot what being a boy was like. And he looked for that boy in others: "I found that whenever I met a stranger I had an inclination to seek beneath his adult lineaments for the face he'd had as a boy. When I can see the boy's face beneath the man's I'm fairly sure that I know what sort of a person he really is."[36]

If we read *Penrod* with enough care, we may catch a long ago and ruefully amusing glimpse of ourselves.

♦ ♦ ♦ ♦ ♦ ♦ ♦ ♦ ♦

MY OWN FAVORITE PULITZER WINNER, WRITTEN IN 1921, is *Alice Adams.* Two scenes from it are unforgettable to me, possibly because as a female I can very unwillingly identify with Alice. In fact, one critic wrote at the time that Booth Tarkington knew more about the feminine heart than any man had a right to know.

Alice, who is from a family of small means, is pathetically and relentlessly pushed by her social-climbing mother towards Society-with-a-capital-*S* and everything that it implies — power, position, and wealth. Near the beginning of the book, Alice attends a dance given by the prominent parents of a rich and beautiful young girl who has the heritage Mrs. Adams covets for Alice. Since she has no escort, her brother, Walter, under duress, takes her, then abandons her while he gambles with the servants. Sitting on the sidelines in a dress that is all wrong, Alice wears a corsage of wilting violets which she has picked that morning and waits for a partner who does not appear. She must have had that expectant look frozen on her face which is meant to tell everyone that her beau has just gone to get her some punch and will be right back, but which fools no one. I would wager that every woman from sixteen to sixty who has gone to dancing school, dances, or balls has shared, if not the anguish — and it is anguish — of Alice, then at least has experienced twinges of worry.

Alice is eventually rescued by the hostess's cousin, and the evening is partly saved. He subsequently calls on her, they go on walks together, and a mild summer romance flowers. The time comes, though, when he must have some time with her family.

The dinner party Mrs. Adams gives for him is a total disaster from start to finish. (For me it is the most terrible party in the history of literature.) Imagine a July evening in Indiana with no fans, no air conditioning, and too much unappetizing food piled high on every plate. The hostess and her daughter make desperate and brittle conversation, pretending that everything is just lovely, while everyone drips with perspiration. (My father claimed he never again could eat a brussel sprout after reading about them in this scene.) Alice knows that after this evening she will never see the young man again. And she never does.

◆ ◆ ◆ ◆ ◆ ◆ ◆ ◆ ◆

UNCLE BOOTH HAD ALWAYS BEEN A VOCAL FOE OF materialism, bigness, the search for power no matter what the consequences, and the ills and heartaches that can come from the scramble for the dollar. Some of his major novels are variations of this theme. Although he never preached, his characters and plots illustrate his strong feelings and echo some of the heartrending as well as fortuitous consequences of our nation's transformation from an agrarian to an industrial economy. For a while he had a captive audience, one reason being that he knew his readers. The critics, however, were getting restive about his work. They wanted "realism," and though his books of social criticism are certainly realistic, he chose to inform by skillful implication and refused to wallow in biological detail. He wrote to Heywood Broun, " 'We are not necessarily ignorant of what we ignore in art.' "[37]

Despite the dissatisfaction of the critics and the havoc of the Depression, his books and short stories continued to bring him considerable income in the thirties. He said of that period, "If I keep reminding myself that I'm the sole support of eleven people, my conscience doesn't hurt quite as much."

He certainly seemed to regard his critics in a very sensible way. He wrote to Erwin Panofsky, a world famous art historian, on March 8, 1945:

> *Artur Rubenstein and I were vis-a-vis at dinner the other*
> *night and one of the lively things he said was that the audience*
> *creates its own concert – all he can do is to give it the*
> *opportunity. To any reader a book is what he brings to it and a*
> *long while ago I became inured to what newspaper reviewers*
> *usually hurried and always innocently judgmatical brought to*
> *works of mine.*[38]

Maybe, however, he also recalled the warning that William Dean Howells had given him in 1899 about the power of the critics: " 'They can still hurt you — long, long after their last power to please you is gone.' "[39]

Uncle Booth had a close friend who certainly should have won some sort of prize for being the most reluctant critic there ever was. It is necessary to backtrack just a bit. When Uncle Booth was a boy, James Whitcomb Riley was one of his sister's beaux. In his autobiography, my uncle wrote, "His manner with my sister, like hers with him, was of the liveliest mock coquetry; they were having a tremendous affair in which there was nothing — nothing but gaiety." When Uncle Booth was twelve and thirteen years old, Riley treated him as an adult, even advising him about his drawings. In fact, at Riley's request, he contributed a little imp on the cover of the poet's first book, *The Boss Girl.* He wrote of Riley, "No other boy could ever have had precisely just such a friend."[40]

After Uncle Booth had had a book published, even after he had become an established writer, he waited in vain for some comments from his friend. But there was only silence, a silence that Uncle Booth did not break, though they often saw each other. He waited for fifteen years! Then one day the poet came to see him and said, " 'I read your new novel. I've come to tell you what I think of it.' " Uncle Booth wrote, "Fifteen years! — but the blessed man came as soon as he could. . . . benison was bestowed the first instant that it could be an honest one."[41] I can scarcely believe my uncle's words. He must, it seems to me, have seen Riley in a golden light. Fifteen years!

Some time before this, my grandmother had asked James Whitcomb Riley to be my father's godfather, and he had agreed. He even wrote an unpublished poem for the occasion, a la Robert Burns — "John Jameson, My Jo-John."

◆ ◆ ◆ ◆ ◆ ◆ ◆ ◆ ◆

BEFORE UNCLE BOOTH'S HEALTH BECAME TOO FRAIL, THE Tarkingtons used to be "at home" on Sunday afternoons. Because of Uncle Booth's rigorous work schedule, they saw only the family during the week, and then in the evening. Friends, visiting celebrities such as the Lunts, Helen Hayes, George Ade, Robert Sherwood, Otis Skinner, Alexander Woollcott and others, as well as neighbors and family, used to drop in Sunday for tea and *real* conversation while

Aunt Susanah presided elegantly behind the huge silver teapot. When my cousin Mig and I were old enough, we were occasionally asked "to pour" — a great honor we thought.

One Sunday, though, even Aunt Susanah's calm was threatened when the four Marx brothers with their wives arrived — separately and in line — each one in a gleaming white Cadillac with a liveried chauffeur at the wheel. The four shining white cars in the driveway must have given the neighbors some interesting speculations. During the visit, Chico turned to Harpo and asked (and I wish I could imitate his accent), "Who does Mrs. Tarkington remind you of?" The answer came without hesitation, "Mama." Aunt Susanah gracefully accepted the heartfelt compliment. Uncle Booth later reported to us that Groucho, cigar in his mouth, had said to him *sotto voce* and with a wink, "I betcha you never had so many Jews in your house."

It was not in Aunt Susanah's nature, as they now say, to "put down" anyone, particularly if the person in question were masculine. This was made quite evident one Christmas Eve a few years before her death in 1966. Her neighbor who was a thoroughly nice man, but a diamond-in-the-rough, brought her a poinsettia plant. He apologized for his failure to call on her sooner saying, "I've had this pain in my butt," and he lifted his jacket to point to the offending part of his anatomy. Smiling as if she had received a *bon mot* from Dr. Samuel Johnson himself, she inclined her head and said in a sweet voice, "Indeed." It was unfortunate that my eyes and those of her brother-in-law met at that instant, and only Providence averted our disgrace.

◆ ◆ ◆ ◆ ◆ ◆ ◆ ◆ ◆

To our generation Uncle Booth was perfect, but our parents knew better. There was occasional tension in the Tarkington household. Uncle Booth was a tease, and his sister-in-law, Louise Keifer, who lived with them, was a natural target. She was a handsome but neurotic woman, who was always beautifully dressed. My father said that when she was young she was stunning. She had had over the years some "gentlemen callers," even one or two serious beaux. But Uncle Booth used to make fun of them to her, and she lost any interest she might have had in them. Poor Aunt Louise was a bit of a scapegoat, I am afraid. Teasing is like sarcasm. There is no defense against either. She did have one beau, though, that I am positive Uncle Booth never made fun of. It was his beloved friend, Julian Street. He admired Louise greatly, and they carried on quite a correspondence for some time. I do not know whether this was before Street was married or after he became a widower. I rather doubt that Aunt Louise could have been happily married to anyone because of her eccentricities. Anyway, the friendship or flirtation seemed to die a natural death.

Aunt Susanah was always the peacemaker. She loved and understood her sister. Aunt Louise was, I think, a tragic woman. Home for her was with the Tarkingtons; but as far as I know, she never had any outside interests. Just once she made suggestions about moving to a place of her own but was easily dissuaded.

Aunt Susanah was much more than a beautiful wife and peacemaker. She managed the household with efficiency and tact, seemingly without effort, protecting Uncle Booth from interruptions and diplomatically dealing with a flow of visitors. Her niece once said she was a "gentle dragon." When Uncle Booth was hard at work, he said he lived a hermit's life. Aunt Susanah saw to it that a basket with food and coffee was put outside the closed door of his workroom each evening.

She also managed the family business affairs, which were considerable, and occasionally murmured at a new art purchase. I remember once being at an art museum exhibit with Uncle Booth when he bought an ancient Javanese head. On the way home, he said to me, "I don't think we'll tell Aunt Susie about this and maybe she won't notice it for a while."

I am sure that when Uncle Booth made the yearly move from Indianapolis to Seawood, or the other way around, he walked into a house in which the fires were lit, the paintings in place, and flowers in profusion on the polished tables. Aunt Susanah did literally anything that was necessary to free Uncle Booth from any fuss or cares. Once he told an inquiring reporter that the only thing he did for himself was shave, and even then, she changed the razor blades.

Aunt Susanah did much more than change razor blades. Once her doctor insisted that she enter the hospital for an operation. Uncle Booth was working almost around the clock to meet a deadline, and she would not have worried him for anything in the world. She announced to the family that she was going to Chicago to visit her sister, Isabel. Then, Aunt Susanah sent to Isabel a packet of letters for Uncle Booth, one of which was to be mailed each day from Chicago. Mattie, the Tarkingtons' beloved cook, was in on the secret. My aunt and she made all the household arrangements together, and Mattie was the person in the household who knew where Aunt

Susanah was. She admitted herself to the hospital, had the operation, and came home in two weeks. (I do not know when this happened, but it was evidently before a person picked up the telephone for a long distance call.) I do not know when or if she ever told Uncle Booth, but the story leaked out because my father told me. Nor do I know what kind of surgery she had. She would have thought it much too indelicate to mention that. Her effort to shield my uncle from worry may sound incredible, but I was not surprised when I heard it. Uncle Booth had a very nearly perfect wife, and the longer they were together, the more he realized it.

My mother was with Aunt Susanah when in her late eighties she had another hospital experience. She was to stay overnight to have a small skin cancer removed. Mother was going to take care of the paperwork always inevitable when one enters a hospital. As they entered the lobby, my mother said, "Aunt Susanah, the form will ask how old you are." She drew herself up to her full five feet plus two or three inches and said firmly, "Florence, no one who has any manners at all asks a lady her age after she is eighty!"

As a child, one usually goes though a period of "I hate my name." I never could join in, because I was so proud to be Aunt Susanah's namesake.

◆ ◆ ◆ ◆ ◆ ◆ ◆ ◆ ◆

AFTER A BATTLE WITH BLINDNESS AND MORE THAN A dozen eye operations in the late twenties and thirties, Uncle Booth did regain partial vision in one eye, but then the household became even more complicated. Aunt Susanah had to be chatelaine of an establishment in which three women were in love with the same man. Before his critical eye trouble, Aunt Louise had done Uncle Booth's typing for him and had been his secretary. But his failing eyesight later required someone who could take dictation. His new secretary, Betty Trotter, a Maine neighbor and friend, became part of the Tarkington household, and she lived with them until his death. Aunt Louise was so jealous that if she had been a murdering sort of person Betty would long ago have been dead. Aunt Louise sniped at her, but Betty usually laughed, which infuriated Aunt Louise even more. Aunt Susanah, though, remained always perfectly serene. She knew very well that Betty was almost in a literal sense Uncle Booth's eyes; and knowing how dependent on Betty's services and devotion he was, she always tried to calm the waters.

Uncle Booth told me once that the hardest thing he ever had to do — and he had had to do some hard things — was to learn how to dictate to a secretary instead of writing down his thoughts in longhand. He said that he had tried several very competent secretaries but was always uncomfortably aware of their waiting presence. Betty, he said, had the quality of seeming to absent herself entirely, so that his concentration was not spoiled by the consciousness of another person. Betty told me once he would be silent for as much as an hour while he searched for just the right word.

I know now that his dependence on Betty was at times difficult for Aunt Susanah, but the surface she presented was one of untroubled serenity. She wanted his needs to be filled even if she had a price to pay. She left Uncle Booth once, possibly a trial separation, but I was not ever aware of this as a child. My father thought she was trying to decide whether to make the separation a permanent one, but he may have been wrong. When Uncle Booth begged her to come back, saying he needed her very much, she did return; and as they grew older, they became closer and closer.

I never saw her serenity and courage break, not even when Uncle Booth was dying. Once my father and I went to see her when Uncle Booth was very ill. Daddy put his arms around her and asked, "Aunt Susanah, how are *you*?" She replied without even a break in her voice, "As well as I can be, John, for someone who has a broken heart."

In Aunt Susanah's code one did not weep. I saw her cry only once. It was the morning of Uncle Booth's funeral. The house was so full of flowers that they overflowed into three other rooms besides the living room. Someone, my father I think, had put one floral tribute on the top of Uncle Booth's coffin. It was a wreath of ivy from Uncle Booth's Princeton club, the Ivy Club. Someone brought Aunt Susanah downstairs, and at the sight of the small, simple message of recognition and condolence, the dam broke — but only briefly. Although her grief was excruciating, she bore it regally, and she expected the same from everyone else when in public.

On that day a motorcycle policeman was on duty at the end of the long driveway; and she, whose life was spent in thinking about other people, sent me out with an invitation for him to come in for a cup of coffee. I have never seen a more surprised man. "I've been on the force a long time," he said, "but this is the first time anyone asked me into the house."

Several years after Uncle Booth's death, my husband and I escorted Aunt Susanah to a large reception given for the engagement

Top: *At Seawood in 1922, Tarkington reads to* (left to right) *his sister, Hautie; his daughter, Laurel; his sister-in-law, Louise Keifer; and his wife, Susanah.* Lower left: *The tragic Laurel at fifteen.* Above: *Louise Keifer, sister of Tarkington's wife, at thirty-five; her home was with the Tarkingtons.*

of a young member of the family. During the party a nice-looking middle-aged woman approached me and said, "Isn't that Mrs. Tarkington with you?" I replied that it was, and she told me that her first employment after nursing school was as Laurel Fletcher Tarkington's private nurse. After the divorce Laurel had lived with her mother who subsequently remarried and had another child. I do not know whether Laurel was already ill or not, but I have heard that after the birth of the new baby she began to act destructively, and I think the parents must have feared for the baby. Her mother sent Laurel to live with Aunt Susanah and Uncle Booth with their full approval. Her illness was diagnosed as dementia praecox, now called schizophrenia. Her father would not hear of her being hospitalized, so this young nurse was employed to help take care of her. I cannot now remember the nurse's exact words, as she and I sat away from the crowded party, but the message came through loud and clear. It was that Aunt Susanah was a saint.

The nurse said she knew we cherished Uncle Booth's memory, but that Mrs. Tarkington was, for her at least, a heroine during this dreadful time. The nurse told me further that Aunt Susanah had shown great courage with Laurel. Once Laurel had broken a hand mirror and come threateningly towards Aunt Susanah with a piece of jagged glass in her hand. Aunt Susanah had just smiled at her, not retreating an inch, and had said, "Now, Laurel, you must give that to me." In the presence of such calmness, Laurel's incipient violence had subsided.

Sudden mood changes were not uncommon in her. The poor child, when she was sixteen, was too quick for Aunt Susanah and the nurse. They were both in the room when she jumped out the second-story window. The fall did not kill her, but the shock and following pneumonia did.

Laurel's nurse may not have given enough credit to Uncle Booth during this awful time. I am sure from what older members of the family have said that Uncle Booth and Aunt Susanah both did their utmost to save Laurel. When Uncle Booth wrote to his friend George Tyler that she had died, the heartbroken father said, " 'Oh, such a brave and bright and gentle spirit! . . . Old friend, you must not grieve for her or for me. . . . I think she went *somewhere* and that a day will come when I shall find her and she'll know all I've wanted so long to be to her.' "[42] He had said when he was divorced by Louisa that it would "kill Laurel." Maybe it did.

Aunt Susanah did not speak of Laurel much, and she certainly never told me anything about the times Laurel's nurse had spoken of, but, then, it was like her not to do so. She was always a listener and a giver, and she very rarely ever spoke of any bad times in her life, at least not to me. I doubt if she spoke of unhappy times to anyone. As I have said, if there was one trait that Aunt Susanah disliked more than any other, it was complaining.

Sometimes, because I was curious, I used to ask her about her first marriage and the years that she lived in England. She had married an Englishman who went to the Boer War and never came back. After the prescribed number of years, he was declared legally dead, and she returned to Dayton. Her invariable answer to my questions was, "That was in my other life." She did tell me, though, that she arrived back in Dayton with very little money and two younger sisters to support. At that time, she said, impecunious single women had to be content with giving music lessons or teaching a little French. She, however, shocked her friends in Dayton and was severely criticized because she went into the insurance business. I only recently learned that a man who had been a great friend of her father's was worried about her finances and advised her strongly to go into insurance, adding that he would give her all his business. His name was John Patterson, founder, owner, and first president of the National Cash Register Company. The Tarkingtons kept in touch with her first husband's family, and once some of her in-laws by her first marriage spent the summer in Maine with them.

◆ ◆ ◆ ◆ ◆ ◆ ◆ ◆ ◆

SOMETIMES WE PLAYED A GAME AT THE TARKINGTONS' similar to what other families called charades. But to us it was simply "The Game," and this is how we played it. The group of people in the room was divided into two teams, one always captained by Betty and the other by Uncle Booth, both of whom had written famous quotations on slips of paper. The captains held the slips, but the team members could see what their captain had written. Each team member in turn — one on one team, then one on the other — received a quotation from the opposing captain, then acted it out for his or her team members. Any actions were permitted; also, props could be used, but absolutely no words. Time was kept to verify which team used the less time to guess the pantomimed quotations. Each team's efforts were added up at the end of The Game, so there were two totals of time spent. Of course, the team using the less time won. The actor could indicate on his fingers how many words were in the quotation and which word he would act out, or he could indicate that he would act the entire quotation at once. We took The Game very seriously, and no quarter was asked or given.

Did Uncle Booth manage us a bit? Maybe. But he was a famous playwright, and we were all too willing actors. Show-offs is probably a better word. The children could, once in a while, parade a little book learning, thereby gaining Uncle Booth's instant admiration — and we dearly loved to please him. It is not because I have an exceptional memory that those evenings of The Game remain so clearly in my mind. When you are having fun, you are making happy memories, and that is what we did so long ago. They have simply stuck in my mind as happy times will.

In Uncle Booth's later years, possibly failing eyesight or general frailty prevented his performing, but he always took a very active part in guessing and thinking of difficult quotations. However, our family remembers one particular evening at the Woodstock Club of Indianapolis after dinner when we were the only guests in the huge living room. Uncle Booth received his quotation and indicated that he would do the entire quotation at once instead of word by word. He quite literally drifted to a far corner of the room where he looked, oh, so lonely. Someone guessed it at once: "I wandered lonely as a cloud."

I remember even now two moments of triumph I had during The Game. Once a member of my team was valiantly, but unsuccessfully pretending to beat a horse. I had just been studying *Hamlet,* and I said very tentatively, "Let the galled jade wince. Our withers are unwrung." Uncle Booth shouted, "Hurrah for Susie!" Some forty odd years later I still remember my glow of happiness.

Game parties occasionally precipitated fearful fights. Once Aunt Susanah received a quotation written by Uncle Booth who, when he thought he could get away with it, slipped in a quotation in a foreign language — a strictly forbidden practice. It was *"Ach du lieber Augustine."* She did a halfhearted folk dance, but, of course, no one guessed it and her time ran out. (Each actor had five minutes to make his or her team guess what the quotation was.) When we on her team yelled, "No fair, you can't have a foreign language," Uncle Booth took a piece of paper, wrote on it, then with a wicked grin gave it to my cousin Mig, saying, "This is in English." His quotation read, "T'was brillig and the slithy toves did gyre and gimble in the wabe." Mig looked dumbfounded at this treachery, then suddenly, before she had even attempted to tell us how many words were in

the quotation, I called out the correct answer. Uncle Booth, out-
raged, accused us of lipreading, using hidden signals, and sharing a
kind of supraliminal communication which excluded other people.
We could not deny his third charge; we called one another "Kindred
Spirit."

Once my little sister, Florence, received the accolade. She really
was little, too, about ten or eleven, I would guess, and that is little
for The Game. After getting her quotation, she cantered around the
room, pretended to get her hair caught in something, and fell down
on the floor. Uncle Booth said wonderingly, "Absalom, my son!" and
he was right, of course. He was nearly struck dumb by the perspica-
city and Bible knowledge in a child.

Do we sound smart? We were not. We were not anything special,
but we were always stimulated by Uncle Booth and tried hard to
show off for him.

Uncle Booth always saw to it that my Uncle Donald received a
quotation from Roman literature. When he received his slip of paper,
Uncle Donald preceded his acting by rolling up his pants and undo-
ing his garters. He never explained why. Maybe he thought that
falling-down-socks and rolled-up trouser legs gave a toga-like appearance; but each time he began this ritual, Uncle Booth leaned
forward and nearly cried with mirth. One of his characteristics was
that he always leaned forward when he laughed. Uncle Donald was
the most completely unselfconscious man I have ever known, and
his serious mien only added to Uncle Booth's amusement.

The novelist Kenneth Roberts was Uncle Booth's good friend
and neighbor in Maine. To enable family members to see Roberts's
temper in action, Uncle Booth introduced him to The Game. Roberts
was a choleric man when he was in *good spirits,* which was not
often. We were not disappointed. His quotation was, "Richard is
himself again." He could have pretended to be a king, and someone
would have eventually guessed the name *Richard.* Or he could have
done the word *himself* without too much trouble. But Roberts never
seemed to realize that the key words were the ones to act first. So he
decided to do *again,* by pulling his foot back and forth on the rug.
When his team was understandably backward, he began to get red in
the face as Uncle Booth had predicted. He just renewed his efforts,
now stamping his foot up and down, and finally shouting, "Use the
bean, dammit!"

Roberts was present at another Game evening in Maine when
Mig and I were there. He received a very unfortunate title as his
quotation: *Caesar's Gallic Wars.* He bellowed with fury, then decided

to act out *Gallic* but did it as *garlic,* a word close to *Gallic* in pronunciation, confident that a member of his team would grasp the
tenuous connection. Of course, no one did, though I am sure he
thought he was acting with convincing clarity. He grew more and
more angry as he stamped around the room depicting a person
smelling garlic by holding his nose and making horrible faces. And
he was a stamper *ne plus ultra.* His team guessed "smelly," "nose,"
"odoriferous," and as his temperature rose, they started saying, "angry," "furious," "temper," and other related words. Uncle Booth was
the only one who knew the quotation since he had made it up, and
seldom has a man enjoyed himself more. Finally, Mr. Roberts "blew"
the way an oil well gushes in. He yelled, "Goddamn you sons of
bitches," to his frustrated and by now intimidated team members;
and with a red fist about the size of a ham, be began pounding with
rage on a delicate Chippendale table on which stood an exquisite
seventeenth-century lamp with rows of delicate teardrop-shaped
mauve prisms. The lamp jumped, the prisms jangled, and the ladies
present remonstrated nervously. Uncle Booth, finally recovering
from his laughter, said mildly, "Don't break the lamp, Ken. Lord Nelson and Lady Hamilton dined by its light."

◆ ◆ ◆ ◆ ◆ ◆ ◆ ◆ ◆

WE USED TO HAVE DINNER AS A FAMILY AT THE TAR-
kingtons' at least once a week, and memories are still vivid. The
dining room was lit by candelabra, as well as by a fire burning under
a black, carved, wooden Roman mantel. On the table lay service
plates. Imagine, empty plates that were removed before any food
was put on them! And spinach that tasted delicious. I realize now it
must have been a molded spinach mousse with béchamel sauce. Not
the least of Aunt Susanah's star qualities was her ability to find and
retain for years and years a cook whose talents were superb.

Mainly I remember dessert: no matter what the season, home-
made vanilla ice cream topped with fresh strawberries was served in
a large silver bowl, and on one side of the mounded ice cream were
always a few marrons. I tasted a marron one night and decided that
marrons were delicious. It was a long time before I realized that the
strawberries were for everyone else and the marrons for Uncle
Booth. Gilmore, the beautiful, tall, black butler who served the dessert, always put the strawberries towards me, but I awkwardly
wielded the heavy, baroque silver serving spoon so that I could

scoop up some marrons for my plate. Uncle Booth, the perfect host, said never a word, though he undoubtedly, even with his bad eyesight, could see that his portion of the delicious brandied chestnuts was unusually small. Finally I realized that Gilmore's almost imperceptible gesture with his head meant, "Take strawberries."

As Gilmore served coffee, Figaro, the poodle, who usually sat in the window seat during dinner, jumped down as if by a hidden signal and sat looking hopefully at Uncle Booth, who always said, "Are you feeling pious?" Figaro then ran to a chair, put his front paws on the seat, and bowed his head. The ensuing dialogue usually went something like this:

> Uncle Booth: Are you a miserable sinner?
> Figaro: A low whine.
> Uncle Booth: ARE YOU A MISERABLE SINNER?
> Figaro: A louder whine.
> Uncle Booth: Did you vote for Franklin Delano
>   Roosevelt?
> Figaro: A contrite groan.
> Uncle Booth: Do you repent of your sin?
> Figaro: A howl of misery.
> Uncle Booth: Amen.

At this word, Figaro, released from confession, came running for his reward of a dog biscuit. We heard this and variations of it many times, but it never failed to delight us. Once my brother and I tried to teach our tired old Airedale to do this trick, but were unsuccessful.

Uncle Booth had standard black poodles long before I was born and took his pets everywhere with him. He often said that they were made of "black sunshine" and once told us the story of being in a Paris bar with Gamin (Gammy) when he said the dog literally stopped a fist fight. Two angry drunken men were battling, and Gammy stood on his hind legs between the pugilists, pawing them with his forepaws, barking anxiously, and wagging his tail. The participants stopped fighting and collapsed in laughter at the unusual referee.

◆ ◆ ◆ ◆ ◆ ◆ ◆ ◆ ◆

DURING ALL MY MEMORIES OF UNCLE BOOTH, GILMORE was present — a constant friend in my life. He took care of "Figo," as we called Figaro, and Uncle Booth told us with great amusement of a conversation he had overheard between the two of them. At the end of the interchange, Gilmore had said fondly, "Man, you is sure some dog."

Many years later I occasionally just had to do errands without the company of my small baby. I used to call Gilmore, who was always delighted to baby-sit. During her nap time, I would leave Susie, a tiny baby, in her basket on the sunny, spacious back porch. I did not even ask the Tarkingtons. They would have acquiesced, but Aunt Louise would have seen it as an imposition on Gilmore. When I returned, I usually found Gilmore in an old rocking chair in the kitchen holding the baby and crooning to her. Since he probably had silver to shine or other chores to do, his workday was lengthened by his kindness to me. It still hurts my conscience that I never even offered to pay him. But then our relationship was that of good friends. A bottle of spirits for Christmas was my substitute for a sitter's fee, and he graciously accepted it.

Gilmore was part of the magic of the Tarkington household. I will always be glad I knew him so well. He was tall, handsome, and very black. My father said once he thought Gilmore must be pure Zulu. He was deeply devoted to Uncle Booth; and if he occasionally made a little trouble "below stairs" because of his reluctance to get Seawood ready for the Tarkington's occupancy each spring, Aunt Susanah handled the matter tactfully and without a word to Uncle Booth. In these days, being a domestic servant is sometimes considered demeaning. But if someone had patronized Gilmore — well, the mind boggles at the thought. He might not have been familiar with the word *patronized,* but he would have sensed the act quickly enough. Gilmore was as proud of his employment as he was of his employer. He was much more than a servant. He was a caring friend who constantly watched over Uncle Booth to see how he could be of help to him — always making sure plenty of his special cigarettes were in the silver case by his chair, his lighter was always filled, the fire was burning perfectly, and the lights were turned on over the paintings at dusk. The night Uncle Booth died I came into the house through the kitchen, and Gilmore and I cried in each other's arms. During Uncle Booth's final illness, Gilmore nursed him tenderly around the clock. Towards the end, though, a trained nurse was in residence, much to Gilmore's resentment.

Figaro

Top: *In the dining room of the Tarkington's Meridian Street house in Indianapolis, Susie indulged in her fondness of marrons.* Left: *Gilmore, the Tarkingtons' friend and butler, stands at the entrance to Seawood with the author.* Above: *A silhouette of Figaro, who, according to Gilmore, was "sure some dog."*

On the sad day when Uncle Booth's coffin was returned to the house for the funeral services, it was necessary for a family member to identify the body in the presence of a mortuary official. Gilmore joined me and my father and the nurse when the coffin was briefly opened. I think he came to tell Uncle Booth goodbye. Tears glistening on the black cheeks, Gilmore said in a suspicious growl, "Where's his rings?" Uncle Booth always wore a gold wedding ring and a signet ring. The nurse said to him gently, "I gave them to Mrs. Tarkington."

After my husband had come back from two years in Europe during World War II, Gilmore told me that since he had never given us a wedding present, he would help us give a party. He did, and the service, of course, was impeccable. But during his work in my kitchen, he had discovered with horror that my flat silver, most of it unpolished, was jumbled up in a drawer with the cooking utensils. Long after the last guest had left and the last glass had been washed, Gilmore sat at the kitchen table, muttering sadly and polishing our silver. He put it away, I remember, with the spoons and forks in little stacked nests, back into the kitchen drawer. Our post-World War II budget hardly ran to a butler's pantry.

Once Frank, my husband, and I were invited to call on Gilmore and his lovely wife, Veida, who also worked for the Tarkingtons. They lived above the garage, but any thoughts you may entertain about "above the garage" apartments must stop right here. Their quarters were an extension, it seemed, of the Tarkington house and had been decorated by Veida. Their home also contained some Tarkington treasures. We were offered a drink of Scotch, the price of which was far beyond what we could afford.

After Uncle Booth's death, Gilmore and Veida continued to work for Aunt Susanah. Gilmore later became very ill, and Aunt Susanah discovered that the hospitals were reluctant to give a black person a private room. So he stayed at home. She had him moved into the room next to hers, and she sat and held his hand the day he died.

♦ ♦ ♦ ♦ ♦ ♦ ♦ ♦ ♦

LONG BEFORE UNCLE BOOTH'S DEATH, ONE OF THE great-nephews remarked upon Uncle Booth's "passionate mind." It may seem a strange adjective to use, but it really is not, not to anyone who knew anything about Booth Tarkington. He had a brilliant mind and was an articulate person who was eager to share his knowledge — especially with great-nieces and great-nephews. In addition, he never talked down to anyone or "showed off" his brilliance. Only infrequently did I even partially plumb the depths of his knowledge of things artistic or literary; and nearly every time I did it, I had an ulterior motive.

The first time was during a Christmas vacation when I was in college, and I had been required to write a paper on Benvenuto Cellini during the holidays. I called the Tarkingtons to see whether I could come over to talk to Uncle Booth about Cellini. "To talk to" is not entirely correct. I wanted to find out about the artist without having to go to the bother of a lot of library research. I was cordially invited to come over one Sunday afternoon for coffee and discussion. Notebook in hand, I walked there through softly falling snow. Uncle Booth's secretary, Betty, was also present, and to use a cliché, the fur flew. Betty, brilliant herself, was the only one of us who ever "talked back" to Uncle Booth, and she did so with spirit that afternoon. They argued, they interrupted each other, they almost yelled at each other about Cellini, his merits as an artist, his morals, his era, and his influence. That day I was exposed to two of the finest minds I have ever known. They forgot, I think, that I was there, and well they might, for I said never a word. I was too busy writing down their violently contrasting ideas. There was such a depth and wealth of materials that I could not get it all down, but I got enough to receive an *A* on the paper, and without any actual library research. It was bald-faced cheating because I did not say in my bibliography, "Conversation between Mr. Tarkington and Miss Trotter." I skidded home in the dusk after this memorable afternoon, feeling like the luckiest girl in the world. I now grieve that I, and possibly we, took this tremendous knowledge and brilliance for granted. He was Uncle Booth, and knowledge, as far as we were concerned, just went with him.

Long after his death, he helped me again when I was a teacher of college English. Because of him, I was able to communicate the genius of Henry James to my students. When I was in college, I had to read *Portrait of a Lady;* and though I was naive about literature in those days, I did sense there was more to James than met the eye, or at least than met my eye. So I questioned Uncle Booth about James, and this is what he wrote to me:

> Portrait of a Lady — *not read for so long that I've forgotten every bit of it, but it's a masterpiece of its period and it's by Henry James and that's enough. You won't find any vulgarity in it, no vulgar writing. It's all of a distinguished texture, and it is*

*done from the upper view. In the upper view the writer produces
the impression that he just reveals his people to you; seemingly
their thoughts, characters, and actions are their own. He doesn't
manipulate events for their benefit. He holds to the truth of them
and what would happen to them. You are not invited to step
upon the stage and be one of them yourself.*

*In the lower type of novel or play the author asks you to
become his principal person — which is the reason that most of
the "heroes" and "heroines" of the romantic novels were made
of impossible perfections. The reader, believing himself perfect,
had to have a perfect "character" to step into — and the youth of
my generation saw even Sidney Carton's drinking as part of his
picturesque perfection. If the reader enjoys his vicarious
experiences, he says the novel is "good" and vice versa, which is
why most men and boys say that our friend Kenneth Roberts is a
"good writer" and why some women say he is "tedious" — and,
of course, neither "verdict" has anything to do with Mr. Roberts's
merits and faults as a writer. In any book of James's you'll find
an inexhaustible curiosity about the nature of a human
being — an untiring analysis of his manifestations and an
incomplete revelation of him for the reason that the whole of
any such being cannot be known to another — or to himself. His
"texture" — his phrasing and sentence structure — you'll find
intricate sometimes; this is usually because he has to say what is
difficult to say.*

*I should think a little observation of "popular prose" would
be useful in English classes with samples from current
magazines. Almost any of them will show the cheap-and-easy
variations upon the simplest and most persistently bothersome
mechanisms of dialogue writing. I don't know what some of the
poor hacks and kids would do without "he nodded" or "John
shrugged," or "the Captain barked," or "snapped" or "growled"
or "Won't you sit down? Mabel invited." For "He said," "He
nodded" has come to be "orfulist." If most of our magazines and
best sellers are to be believed, human conversation is largely
accomplished by necks on greased axles.*[43]

When I was at Smith and my cousin was at Bryn Mawr during
the New Deal era, we were each taking a course in economics. We
carried on a spirited correspondence with Uncle Booth, telling him
earnestly how the world should really be run. He was simply
horrified at what he considered the left-wing garbage we were being
exposed to. His reply to both of us was a textbook on politics and
economics which consisted of about thirty typewritten pages, called

"Notes for Nieces." Among other relevant information, it contained definitions of communism as practiced in Russia and elsewhere; comments on socialism and facism; and some remarks he clearly could not resist making on the condition of America under FDR, who to put it mildly was not his favorite leader. A serious piece written with clarity and knowledge, it contained definitions of terms that some economic professors seem to be vague about and concerned the practical facts of economic life. Two economics professors got the surprise of their lives when Mig and I, having absorbed this information, began questioning our teachers and having our own answers. In "Notes for Nieces," he had not insisted that we think a certain way, but mostly that we think.

Uncle Booth would have been successful in many professions, and teaching was not the least of them. Although I taught college English, not economics, I often took pages of "Notes" to read to students I thought were off the track. I was teaching during the sixties, and my class and I often rambled off the subject. "Notes" was of incomparable help. Uncle Booth's clearly and simply written views offered the misinformed and ill-informed student an alternative to the popular economic perspective of the day. Of course, I never admitted that Uncle Booth's ideas were not my own. I hope his common sense and way of making a complex subject seem logical and easy reached a few of them.

◆ ◆ ◆ ◆ ◆ ◆ ◆ ◆ ◆

TRYING TO RECAPTURE MEMORIES IS A WILL-O'-THE-WISP game. Now you have them. Now you do not. A conscious effort to relive the past is never enough. The senses provide the key to that curious feeling that you have really gone back in time: the half-forgotten bar of music, a certain combination of smells, a familiar voice or smile, the sight of someone's handwriting. Suddenly, without any conscious effort, the past comes into such a clear focus that the present is momentarily as unreal as a dream. For me, rereading the letters Uncle Booth wrote to me when I was in college has sharpened all the memories and has reminded me of the many visits to Seawood. Could unclouded happiness such as I knew at Seawood have ever really existed? I think it did.

In 1938 during my freshman year at Smith College, I thought of myself as a sophisticated woman of the world. Uncle Booth's letter to me before my roommate, Ann, and I went to Kennebunkport for the first time indicated gently that he did not share my opinion. This journey to Maine was to be our first unchaperoned trip by train. I had never stayed in a hotel without a grown-up. If I did not have the sense to realize what was involved in the trip, he did:

> *Most likely both you and Ann would feel there's too much*
> *lonesomeness up here at this season — ocean and woods and*
> *sea gulls and old pictures can be poor company for youth used*
> *to living in crowds. At your age I was at Exeter, and I hardly*
> *dare think what I'd have thought of K'port in late autumn. We*
> *were delighted you had a gay time at Williams and if you're*
> *asked to another dance and game next week, we'll understand*
> *your natural preference, because if positions and age were*
> *reversed, we'd feel the same way — at least your Aunt Susanah*
> *certainly would, and I'm not sure she'd need any reversal of age*
> *to feel that way either! I'm enclosing a check for expenses (you'll*
> *pay Ann's too of course) which would include tickets to Boston*
> *and from there to Kennebunk, parlor car, a double room at the*
> *Ritz Carlton with bath, dinner, and breakfast. You should have*
> *dinner served in your room at the hotel. Be sure to have plenty*
> *of change for tips and tip Pullman porters, station porters, taxi*
> *drivers, waiters, hotel cab starters, luggage porters and dining*
> *car waiters. A dinner tip for two at the hotel would be two*
> *dollars, breakfast tip one dollar [and this was in 1938]. The Ritz*
> *food charges may shock you a little, but you must eat. I think*
> *you'd best not go out to a theater or elsewhere as Boston streets*
> *are rather rowdy and the street crossings are all dangerous. . . .*
> *When you want to order supper you use your room telephone*
> *and call room service and ask for a waiter to be sent to your*
> *room. . . . The train for Kennebunk leaves Boston North Station*
> *at 8:35 in the morning so order your breakfast early and allow*
> *35 minutes to reach the station in a taxi. . . . There! You'd*
> *probably get along just as well without all this avuncular*
> *palavering. Nor do I really want to interfere with any plans you*
> *and Ann may have made for a riot and ptomaine in Boston*
> *Friday night.*[44]

Plans that did risk "riot and ptomaine" had previously been made. Maybe it was expecting too much to ask that, on our own for the first time, we would dine in our room. I think it was horror at the idea of tipping anyone two dollars as much as the allure of Harvard men that caused us to disobey instructions.

The imperturbability of waiters at expensive hotels is legend, but even the impassive calm of the Ritz waiters must have been threatened the morning that Ann and I breakfasted there before catching the early train. We felt that we were much too grand for the

Top: *Tarkington dictates to his secretary Betty Trotter (about 1940).* Left: *Mig and Fenton Jameson, Donald's daughter and son, home on leave during World War II.* Above: *In 1938 Uncle Booth shows his "Kennebunkport look" in the company of* (right) *Susie and* (left) *her college roommate, Ann Notman.*

coffee shop, but the number of waiters and the prices in the dining room made us very nervous. We were the only guests eating that early, and we anxiously noted that *several* waiters were in constant and hovering attendance. When one of them lighted our cigarettes (we did not really want them, but thought smoking added to the appearance of sophistication) and another kept refilling our coffee cups, we were suddenly so overcome with confusion that I tremblingly took Uncle Booth's letter out of my purse; and we studied it carefully. A tip for *every* waiter? We thought they all looked expectant. Where gratuities are concerned, there is no miser like a college freshman. We left a fifty-cent piece and fled.

◆ ◆ ◆ ◆ ◆ ◆ ◆ ◆ ◆

ONCE IN A WHILE, BUT NOT OFTEN, WE ARE FORTUNATE enough to appreciate the perfection of an experience while it is happening. We can treasure every moment, not just in memories, but as we are in the midst of the loveliness. For us, Seawood was a fairyland — a place of enchantment. We were never so young, so carefree, so protected, and so surrounded by exquisite beauty.

Uncle Booth had first gone to Maine in 1903 after a nearly fatal attack of typhoid fever. In fact, he was so ill that his father, hoping to insure his rest, had had a block of the street in front of the house sanded so the sound of the horses' hooves would not disturb him. Much later, Uncle Booth himself told me about coming down with an excruciating headache during a family Sunday dinner. He did not know it then, but it was a symptom of the fever. He had just returned that morning from a stay at French Lick, the spa in southern Indiana which at that time had a large gambling casino next to it where he had lost a great deal of money the night before. His nephews had got wind of his evening either through guessing or eavesdropping and during the interminable meal had yelled repetitively and with maniacal and earsplitting glee, "Uncle Booth lost five thousand dollars! Uncle Booth lost five thousand dollars!"

After the worst of his illness was over, his doctor told him to go to Kennebunkport, Maine, to recuperate, "the healthiest place in the United States." Uncle Booth fell in love with the ocean and pine woods and promised to return there. But before he returned to Maine, he and his wife and his parents went abroad for a year of travel, which lengthened into nine years. It was not until 1917 that he purchased eighteen acres, and Seawood was built. Some people called it the "house that Penrod built," a description that annoyed him, but it may have been true.

Uncle Booth said many times that beauty is better than shekels. Seawood was truly beautiful. It was a very large (or so it seemed to me on that first visit) white colonial, seven-bedroom house, facing the Kennebunk River on the west, fields and woods on the east, and — most exciting for me — from the stairway landing, a view of the Atlantic Ocean. The pillared house fronted on a little wood (partially man-made, I think) and a garden with continuously flowering plants along the paths down to a green lawn with a pond and beautiful stone statue of a maiden. The gravel driveway was flanked by tremendous lilac bushes which were in fragrant bloom when we went to Seawood in June. Even today I cannot smell lilacs without being reminded of those at Seawood, where the perfume mixed with the salt air.

If the Tarkington house in Indianapolis was a muted fairyland, Seawood was a bright, sunny one, situated high on a hill. Its large rooms were airy, alight with sunshine by day and lit by delicate candelabra, French chandeliers, and Wedgwood and Sevres lamps by night. French mantels adorned both the drawing room and the living room. Fires always glowed in the evenings, as Maine nights are chilly. The downstairs was furnished in Heppelwhite, Chippendale, and Sheraton with Aubusson rugs on the floors and portraits by Stuart, Lely, Romney, Raeburn, and Reynolds on the walls in both of the large rooms.

Descending a curved stairway from the sun room, one came to a spacious, lofty, and dark room of which every timber and piece of window glass had been brought from a late Tudor or early Stuart English hunting lodge. Reassembled at Seawood, it became fondly known as the Jacobean Room and formed a wing of the main house. The room was paneled and floored with oak blackened by smoke and time, and its recessed, diamond-shaped window panes were thought by Uncle Booth to be the original seventeenth-century glass. The sun streaming through these panes laid diamonds of sunshine on the planked floor. There were a heavily carved oak fireplace, so large that we could almost walk into it; commodious window seats, where Figaro sat each morning; books in shelves almost to the ceiling; portfolios on the heavy Jacobean tables; a writing desk for Betty; and a comfortable chair for Uncle Booth, for this was where he worked every morning. When Seawood was first built, Uncle Booth worked in the gallery which overlooked the drawing room. Off the gallery was the door to his bedroom, to which he could retreat if guests arrived while he was working. This arrangement proved unsatisfactory, so he adopted the Jacobean Room as his work place because, being a separate wing, it was far from interruptions. Although from a different architectural period than the rest of Seawood, the Jacobean Room seemed exactly right and an integral part of the main body of the house. This ancient room made history come alive for Uncle Booth. He told me once, "Elizabeth and Essex may not have met in this room, but they could have." To another of his nieces, he remarked, "I wonder if Sir Walter Raleigh ever looked through these windows."

Upstairs, the guest rooms which we used were furnished with fine examples of delicate American antique furniture, and the appointments were harmonious — chintz at the windows, antique quilts on the beds, lemon verbena soap in the bathroom. Veida changed the towels and the linen sheets every day. (When I was at Seawood with a friend or my cousin, there were six in the household which meant eighty-four sheets a week to be laundered.)

I went to Seawood many times when I was in college, sometimes with a college friend or my roommate, Ann, often with my cousin Mig. She and I used to visit the Tarkingtons for a couple of weeks before and after our college terms. It was really heaven, or as near to heaven as one can reach in this life. I used to think even then that if something bad had to happen to me I hoped it would be at Seawood. I cannot define what I meant by "bad," but I felt that Seawood could alleviate any kind of suffering. I also saw myself whirling around at a ball given in the drawing room, while musicians in the balcony played Strauss waltzes on stringed instruments. I do not know whether *Mayerling* costumes were even contemporary with Strauss, but that is how I saw everyone dressed. I still think of that daydream when I hear "Wiener Blut" or "The Blue Danube."

Our routines at Seawood gave us free time to be on our own and plenty of time for pleasure with our host. Mig and I breakfasted alone in the dining room, for other members of the family had breakfast in their rooms. Then the morning was ours, and we rarely saw the family until lunch, unless we went shopping in the village with Aunt Susanah. Many of the mornings were spent in exploring. A seacoast holds wonders for the Indiana-born, and we scrambled over the rocky shore.

The family assembled at lunchtime when we discovered gastronomic delights unknown to the midlander. Lunch always included fish, and we were introduced to clams on the half shell, steamed clams, boiled and broiled lobsters, and delicately broiled mackerel. In 1938 lobster was considerably less expensive than hamburger on the Maine coast.

◆ ◆ ◆ ◆ ◆ ◆ ◆ ◆ ◆

WE SPENT MANY HOURS AT THE FLOATS, A TWO-STORIED boathouse about two blocks up the Kennebunk River from the ocean and the same distance down the hill from Seawood. Uncle Booth and William Trotter, Betty's father, had bought the boathouse to give employment to an old sea dog, Capt. Blyn Montgomery, who had had a position at the summer people's fancy and expensive River Club just down the road. Captain Montgomery had been fired without notice, recommendation, or pension because he was not dressy enough for its guests. So he found a safe harbor being caretaker for The Floats.

The contents of the huge first floor of the boathouse were a jumbled treasure trove: bowsprits from whalers that used to set out from Maine ports, cobblers' benches, ship models, canoes and rowboats, a diver's suit, and a sea chest with the maps and uniforms of its long-dead owner. We felt like Robinson Crusoe as we explored. Hanging from the center of the ceiling, a large model of a Spanish galleon which had been wired for electricity lighted the dark room. A Franklin stove surrounded by comfortable deck chairs provided warmth on chilly days. On the river side of The Floats, a deck stood on high stilts to prevent its being inundated by the high tide. On the deck, wicker chairs and warm rugs offered us a place to sit and read or dream as we watched the gulls wheeling, screeching, and prodding for clams at low tide.

The second floor of The Floats was a storage room for American antique furniture, most of which had been purchased and stored there by Betty's mother, but some by Aunt Louise. She, poor woman, must have had a nesting instinct and possibly dreamed of using this furniture in a home of her own.

After my college graduation in 1942, my whole family and Mig visited the Tarkingtons in Maine; and my brother, Mig, and I slept at The Floats which had plenty of beds on the second floor. It was hard to leave the warm fire of Seawood in the evenings and stumble down the hill to The Floats in the blackout. Mig and I cooked our breakfasts in the little galley, but my brother was not enthusiastic about our cooking.

Next to The Floats was a two-masted schooner, the *Regina,* with all her rigging intact. Uncle Booth had bought her in Portland, and she had sailed to the mouth of the Kennebunk River where she ignominiously went aground. Having her moved to a giant cradle in the river by The Floats was a monumental task. Uncle Booth told me that while she was stuck aground the Kennebunkport townspeople called her "Tarkington's folly." Her deck was a good place for sunbathing protected from the wind, and her cabin for exploring and imagining marvelous voyages.

The Floats, where Uncle Booth went nearly every afternoon for coffee and conversation, became a sort of private gentlemen's club, but all were welcome. Dr. Erwin Panofsky described it when he wrote a piece about Uncle Booth and his Maine friendship with him and Aunt Susanah in an article "Humanitas Tarkingtoniana" in 1946:

> *Thus the old boat-house on the Kennebunk River is a curious microcosm, a human universe in a nutshell. It is open to gentlemen retired from the presidency – or the ticket window – of a big railroad, and to the budding actors and actresses of the local summer theatre; to friends so old that they remember, and never tire to recount, the plays performed on Broadway when New York had just received the blessings of electricity, and to friends so new that they have to be initiated into the very rudiments of Kennebunkportian folklore; to students just home from the war of 1945, and to veterans reminiscing about the war of 1898. All these men, women and half-children come to Booth Tarkington with their memories, hopes and sorrows, confiding in him and craving his advice. He talks to all of them and listens to all of them. . . . and there is nothing on earth, from the emotional problems of a freshman to the political problems of the United Nations, from the technique of Gothic glass painters to nuclear physics, from an anecdote about the court of Louis XIV to the way of navigating a whaling ship, that would not hold his interest and stimulate his imagination.*[45]

Mig and I remember when we played Sherlock Holmes at The Floats with Uncle Booth. She and I were the storytellers, the friends of the victim, in the murder case that we made up, and Uncle Booth was Holmes. We retired to the deck of the *Regina* to make up a story of a murder from which Uncle Booth would pick out the clues and which he would then solve. Once we gave him our elaborate mystery story, and he replied, "Captain Bronson [that was always Mig's name in those games], I can tell from your tie that you had egg for breakfast, and what's more you ate it with a fork. Certain jabs in your gums give this away." General hilarity prevented any serious solving of that particular crime.

I say we went to The Floats each afternoon, but occasionally we were tactfully asked to leave for a while when Kenneth Roberts came in for help on his latest novel. Upon our return, we often heard retreating bellows of anguish as Roberts departed after Uncle Booth had encouraged him and then patiently, but firmly, told him he would have to use the scissors and cut out much of what he had written. Evidently his tendency was to overwrite. Uncle Booth gave Roberts such exhaustive and constructive criticism that James Woodress, Uncle Booth's biographer, says he was in a great part responsible for Roberts's success as a novelist. Uncle Booth told Mig and me that Roberts was incomparable at writing of men on forced marches, as in *Northwest Passage,* but could not write a convincing woman's part. We used to find Uncle Booth amused but very sympathetic when we returned to The Floats.

With the unusual generosity that was his hallmark, Uncle Booth counseled Roberts in 1930 as the Tarkingtons waited for a train to take Uncle Booth to Baltimore and Johns Hopkins Hospital during his first terrifying siege of blindness. Roberts remembered that the last thing Uncle Booth did before leaving Maine for the hospital was to dictate "suggestions for using material cut out of *The Lively Lady*."[46]

In the mornings on warm days, Mig and I often took the rowboat or the canoe, paddled across the river, then walked to the beach. We had been warned against going to the mouth of the river because of the strong riptides. Being real landlubbers, we heeded the injunction. We occasionally tried swimming in the ocean, but its iciness in June and September daunted even us. Going into it just knee deep was torture. Sometimes on nice days, we paddled into Kennebunkport in the canoe; because of our origins in landlocked Indiana, we were astonished to discover what it was like to paddle a canoe in a tidal river. We seemed to stay in one spot or to go backwards when we were paddling against the tide; but when the canoe and the tide went in the same direction, the current was so strong that we just steered it and glided swiftly over the water. Once, the sleek head and soft brown eyes of a seal rose from the water right by our vessel, and the creature looked at us solemnly before dropping out of sight.

Top: *Seawood's drawing room where some of Tarkington's portrait collection was displayed.* Above: *The author's bookplate which features the diamond-shaped panes of the window in the Jacobean Room.* Left: *The entrance to Seawood in Kennebunkport, Maine, where the Tarkingtons spent their summers.*

Booth Tarkington

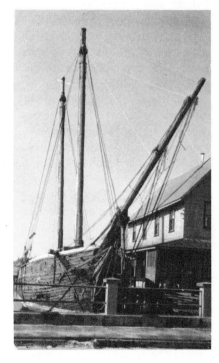

Top: (Left) *Capt. Henry Thirkell piloted the* Zan Tee *which carried Uncle Booth and guests on early afternoon "whale hunts" until World War II began.* Left: *Tarkington's schooner, the* Regina, *cradled next to The Floats.* Above: *A corner of the first floor of The Floats, the boathouse where Uncle Booth and friends enjoyed afternoon coffee and conversation.*

WHEN MIG AND I BEGAN TO GO TO SEAWOOD IN 1938, Uncle Booth still had his forty-five-foot motorboat, the *Zan Tee,* maintained and run by Capt. Henry Thirkell. After lunch on fine days, we would go for rides on the ocean, the *real ocean,* looking for whales. We never saw any, but it was fun watching for spouts which occasionally had been sighted—alas, never when we were on board. Had I been present at such a sighting, I probably would have fallen overboard in my excitement. As it was, the ride was exciting enough. Captain Thirkell, Uncle Booth, and sometimes Betty sat in the stern and talked, but Mig and I always sat in the bow, reveling in the feel of the salt spray, the size of the waves, and the thoughts of adventure. Sometimes we almost left the sight of land, an intoxicating experience for girls brought up where the largest body of water is the White River. Of course, the *Zan Tee* was put up during World War II, so our trips to sea were halted.

After our ocean rides, we would return to The Floats where the coffee and conversation were excellent — sometimes in the company of distinguished guests. Editors from Doubleday were often present. Alfred Lunt and Lynn Fontanne joined the group once, as did Otis Skinner. Alexander Woollcott occasionally came not only to The Floats but also visited at Seawood. Aunt Susanah usually took to her bed when Mr. Woollcott visited, because she strongly disapproved of his manners and his politics. Uncle Booth's art dealer, David Silberman, who is the hero in the *Rumbin Galleries* stories, was also a frequent guest. (Once Mr. Silberman, hoping to ingratiate himself with Uncle Booth, I guess, sent Betty Trotter a quart of Tabu perfume. She gave all the female members of the family about half a cup of the strong stuff. I still remember our aromatic state.) Almost every day, much to Betty's dismay, Francis Noble arrived just in time for coffee. He was a moody ex-newspaperman, who lived in a shack — and it was a real shack — across the river and hated everyone but Uncle Booth. He was what Uncle Booth laughingly called a "gentleman drinker." His breath was redolent of the bottle, and he talked incessantly through the conversation of any guests who might be present, much to Betty's irritation and Uncle Booth's amusement.

About five o'clock we returned to Seawood, where the family members retired to their rooms for a rest. Mig and I went to either her bedroom or mine and read aloud to each other, usually from a book Uncle Booth had recommended. We discovered Maurice Hewlett, whom Uncle Booth greatly admired. He said that Hewlett was a writer's writer, his own favorite book being *The Spanish Jade.* One of his favorite passages concerns a young man who has come to stab a lady who has "wronged" him, but who changes his mind when he sees her in the moonlight: "Tormillo put into Don Luis's hands the long knife. Don Luis threw it out far into the lake. It fled like a streak of light, struck, skimmed along the surface and sank without a splash."[47] Uncle Booth felt that many writers would have overwritten this dramatic passage.

♦ ♦ ♦ ♦ ♦ ♦ ♦ ♦ ♦

THE FAMILY DRESSED FOR DINNER. ON THE DINING ROOM table, more formally set than at lunch, were a damask tablecloth, eighteenth-century silver, old English glass, and in the finger bowls at the end of the meal were nosegays of sweet peas and lemon verbena or geranium leaves. Dinner was nearly always a very pleasant occasion.

I say "nearly always" because occasionally Aunt Louise carped at Betty, who laughed at her, which of course fanned the flames. Or Aunt Louise might accuse Mig or me of having a cold. A slight clearing of the throat was occasion for the accusation, "You have a terrible cold." Once we did get colds, and if we had to cough or blow our noses in our bedrooms, we used to flush the toilet at the same time, since her bedroom was directly across the hall from ours. The Tarkingtons were particularly afraid of colds since Uncle Booth's eye doctor had warned him that the retina in his good eye might detach if he had a spell of coughing.

After dinner and a tour of the paintings, we listened to music or to Betty reading aloud, or sometimes we played The Game with visitors. Uncle Booth had purchased a huge Capehart record player (stereo was then unknown), which stood on the balcony and poured down heavenly music. He always asked any guests what their musical preferences were. (His own favorite composer was Brahms, and the organ his favorite instrument.) Or Betty might read us a chapter of Uncle Booth's latest book or one of his short stories. Betty's reading aloud was fun for us, and I think Uncle Booth used us listeners as a kind of sounding board.

One evening at Seawood, Ann and I were present in body only when Betty read aloud. We were visiting the Tarkingtons after our final exams. Having foolishly and predictably stayed up all the night before to cram, we were very sleepy when we arrived. After dinner while Betty was reading, we both fell sound asleep. Our embarrassment was horrendous when we were awakened in time to go to bed. Uncle Booth was much amused, of course, and guessed why we had fallen asleep. He said that the couch where we had slumbered looked like a stricken battlefield. He added, to make us feel better, "Betty was reading in the voice and tone she uses to read me to sleep, so you can see how effective she is." He always made one feel better after any lapses in behavior.

Uncle Booth's graciousness and sensitivity smoothed our embarrassment on Ann's and my first visit to Seawood. Upon our arrival, we immediately went to The Floats. Uncle Booth, if he wished conversation, was disappointed because Ann and I disappeared, returning, very windblown, in time to be driven back to the house in the late afternoon. We were ashamed of our rudeness, but Uncle Booth, again with understanding, said, "I wondered where you went until I realized that this is the first time either of you had ever seen the ocean and you just had to explore." He was right. We had clambered out to the very end of the breakwater to watch the gulls and the waves.

◆ ◆ ◆ ◆ ◆ ◆ ◆ ◆ ◆

FRANCIS MULBERRY CHICK, ALL 245 POUNDS OF HIM, was Uncle Booth's chauffeur in Maine. Before working for the Tarkingtons, he had been Kennebunkport's only taxi driver. Dr. Panofsky said that Chick thought it was loquacious to blow his horn even if a car were about to back into his own. Chick, at first, declined Uncle Booth's generous offer to be his chauffeur, but acquiesced when Uncle Booth agreed to buy his taxi in addition to Chick's services. However, he refused to have a telephone in his house, saying, "I do enough for them summer people as 'tis." So when his services were needed, someone from Seawood had to go and fetch him. Chick's opinion of the Tarkingtons was well known: " 'We folks around here like the Tarkingtons. They're so common.' "[48] Chick's comments delighted Uncle Booth. He said once to Uncle Booth that he liked his wife because "she treats me like a puffick stranger." Uncle Booth wrote to Dr. Panofsky on June 2, 1945: "Chick is repetitively interested in the rumor that Mrs. Deland left her chauffeur $10,000."[49]

◆ ◆ ◆ ◆ ◆ ◆ ◆ ◆ ◆

WHEN MY ROOMMATE, ANN, AND I VISITED SEAWOOD, IT was during the New Deal era. Uncle Booth was then writing some stories for the *Saturday Evening Post* which were later published in book form as *The Fighting Littles*. When queried about his source for Ripley Little, the main character, Uncle Booth did not bother to deny that, although Ripley was a caricature, he had some obvious characteristics in common with my father. Both were doting, if puzzled, parents whose teenage children with their teenage friends surged around them, acting as if their fathers were invisible. And none of their offspring paid the slightest attention to any parental edicts. My father's other similarity to Ripley was that both had a short fuse on one topic: the Roosevelt administration. Even the mention of FDR caused an explosion. My own father's reactions were strong, but Ripley's were intense. He violently overreacted to any situation that ordinarily would have caused only mild annoyance.

One night at dinner at Seawood, Ann told us a story about her great-uncle John, who was driving in Ontario on a scorching summer day. The one-lane highway was unpaved, and he got trapped behind a barely moving cart that was spreading oil out of pipes from both of its sides to lay some of the dust on the road. Uncle John honked and honked, swore and swore, but the oil-cart driver took no notice. Finally he shouted out of the car window, "If you don't move over, I'm going to knock off all your damn pipes!" Still the cart did not move, but Uncle John did. He roared by the cart, neatly slicing off every pipe on one side. Later, in traffic court the driver told his story to the judge. He ended with, "He was a man of his word. He done it." We all laughed and I, at least, forgot all about the story.

A few months later, I received a telegram from Uncle Booth, dated November 29, 1939. It read: "Please tell Ann to see this week's *Saturday Evening Post* for her story. Love, Uncle Booth." She did, and an enraged Uncle John had become an enraged Ripley Little. Of course, there were some new touches. Ripley, in the story, was driving his family to New England in blistering summer weather. The oil cart became a hay wagon, which Ripley would never have been stuck behind except for the fact that he thought he had taken a short-cut. After screaming and cursing and honking, without the slightest reaction from the driver ahead, he sped by in a fury, taking off a wheel of the hay wagon as he went. He then stopped his car and punched the driver in the stomach. Unfortunately, in his rage he also hit the constable when he arrived. He was the owner of the hay and the brother of the driver of the hay wagon. Ripley did not help his cause by shouting that the hay was green and two-thirds weeds.

After being a guest in the local jail, Ripley rejoined his family, expecting — and knowing he deserved — the proverbial coals of fire. To his incredulity he discovered that his fearful behavior over the haywagon contretemps "had given him a higher stand with his family than he'd ever before attained." His son, Filmer, looked at him with "profound admiration" and worshipful eyes.[50]

People sometimes ask an author where he gets his material, and here is an example. Uncle Booth took a germ from an amusing incident, a couple of characteristics of his nephew, added imagination and some alchemy, and the result was a funny story.

◆ ◆ ◆ ◆ ◆ ◆ ◆ ◆ ◆

THE ADVENT OF AUNT SUSANAH'S BIRTHDAY IN JUNE always occasioned an afternoon trip to an antique shop in Ogunquit run by Messrs. Hare and Coolidge. I am not sure now of its name. We just called it Hare and Coolidge's. It was a *crème de la crème* shop, and Uncle Booth must have been its best customer. I can give some idea of its prices very easily. Once at Seawood, while my husband was overseas in World War II, I wanted to send my sister-in-law a bread-and-butter present. Kitty, I knew, was very fond of Wedgwood, and at Hare and Coolidge's, I saw a lovely little Wedgwood teapot. I asked the supercilious shop attendant how much it cost, and he said, "Three-fifty." To my everlasting humiliation, I extracted three dollars and fifty cents from my purse and asked him to wrap it for me. The only person who was amused was Uncle Booth, who chuckled all the way back to Kennebunkport. I still suffer at the thought of my ignorance.

If Uncle Booth purchased a new *objet d'art* for one of the Seawood rooms, we played a most rewarding game after dinner. Uncle Booth called it "pooning." Pooning consisted of rearranging the lovely art objects on the tables in one of the rooms to make a place for a new purchase. Mig and I used to rearrange without the other one being in the room, and whatever we subtracted from the delicate art objects was usually given to us as a present. Uncle Booth would then arrange his treasures as he undoubtedly planned to do in the first place. (In my house right now, I have some pooning treasures from that time of so long ago.)

In 1923, *The Collector's Whatnot,* a satirical spoof about antique seekers and antique dealers, was published. Uncle Booth used the pseudonym Milton Kilgallen. His coauthors were Kenneth Roberts and Hugh Kahler. They all knew the ignorant avidity of some antique hunters and the unscrupulous wiles of some dealers. They must have had great fun writing it. In the chapter about pooning, the authors wrote, "Many true lovers of the quaint-and-rare possess the patience and means to make collections, but, when it comes to the tasteful *pooning* of these, lack the connoisseur touch that is distinctive."[51] They continued with a list of "don'ts" about pooning; for example: "Don't fasten coat-hangers upon the wall just above valuable water-color paintings. Wet raincoats may cause the colors to run. If your wall space is limited, the hangers should be placed above *oil* paintings." The authors also warned the owners of Boucher pastels not to put them on the same wall with a stuffed moose-head. The place for the latter is over the shower bath where it can be fitted with a nozzle and used as a shower fixture. They deplored the use of "alfalfa as a decoration for mirror-and-picture-frames." It should be placed outside the house where it will be "convenient for the horse" and, anyway, inside the house it produces an effect "too stringy and tends to clutter." They applauded, however, the present tendency to use sumach and cattails in a manner similar to that of "our ancestors under Garfield and Arthur."[52]

I remember that Uncle Booth once said he would give a prize to the girl who could pick out the one furniture reproduction in the living room. Mig and I both guessed wrong, but both got a prize, and also a lesson in how to detect reproductions even if they had been "distressed." Eager dealers sometimes put wormholes and other signs of deterioration on new furniture to confuse the avid and ignorant buyer of antiques.

The Collector's Whatnot describes the methods by which new furniture is distressed. After the new piece is carved, "the manufacturer turns over the product to three or four muscular hirelings whose sole duty is to injure furniture." Using sticks they chastise "the wood with extreme severity. In this way the chests and sideboards acquire, in the matter of half an hour, the scratches and indentations for which slow centuries might otherwise be required."[53] The book continues with a detailed description of the various ways to make wormholes — the crudest being done with a shotgun, but a close investigation by a wormhole collector reveals a No. 10 shot in each hole. The true wormhole craftsmen are Italian: "The Italian worm-holes stand at the very pinnacle of the worm-hole world; and when an antique Italian workman really exerts himself to worm-hole a piece of oak, the French workman stands aside in reverence. The French workman, however, has the dash."[54]

French and Italian methods are compared. Parisian experts press a square plate with a number of thin augers against the wood and make their holes in a cluster, making sure that the wormhole pattern never repeats itself; the Italian uses an irregularly shaped auger to make a "wormy crookedness," thus copying the vagaries of the burrowing worm. According to the authors, the Dutch wormholes of the first quarter of the seventeenth century bear an "unmistakable stigmata" that any buyer, however untutored, should recognize. Because the nervous systems of the worms were greatly affected by the many frosts of that period, the disoriented creatures always "bored to the left in successive *échelons,* or steps and cut into the borings of the worms beyond them." There is a positive test of authenticity for the careful buyer. The dealer has, of course, filled the holes with wood dust. When the purchaser puts his "forefinger over any worm-hole in a given space," places his "lips over the worm-hole next to the left of the obstructed orifice," and then blows into it, "if the hole is a true Dutch hole . . . a small cloud of dust will emerge from the hole next to the one" into which he is blowing, often blinding him temporarily in one eye — "incontrovertible proof that the chest had been in existence in Holland during the first quarter of the seventeenth century . . . acquired by the Pilgrims during their enforced vacation in Leyden before sailing for America in the Mayflower."[55] *The Collector's Whatnot* is a truly delightful *caveat emptor.*

Years later after Uncle Booth had tried to make me somewhat knowledgeable about antiques, I saw what I believed to be a lovely French antique fruitwood chair in a shop. I asked him to look at it before I bought it. He did. He then told the dealer, an old friend of his, that he would publicly expose his fraudulence if the dealer even so much as had the terrible reproduction hidden in his *attic.*

♦ ♦ ♦ ♦ ♦ ♦ ♦ ♦ ♦

AFTER MY COMMENCEMENT EXERCISES AT SMITH, WHEN MY whole family and Mig visited the Tarkingtons for a week, Kenneth Roberts called up one morning in some agitation. Some of his farmhands had quit. He had to get his hay in before a coming storm and could the house party come over and help? The payment for each hayer was to be an autographed copy of a Roberts book. We, except for my father who was wiser than the rest, accepted happily. For me, visions of Merrie England and Constable's "The Hay Wain" ran through my head. We all thought it might be an adventure. We quickly found out one thing we had not realized: haying is very hard work. Maybe the first two or three forkfuls were fun, but when we looked at the huge field awaiting our efforts, our spirits sank. All of us would have liked to have begged off, but pride intervened. It was a very hot, sticky, thundery day, and soon we were dripping wet and itching from pieces of hay that stuck to us. Blisters formed as Roberts pretended to be Simon Legree.

After an eternity, our overseer announced that we could take a rest and that he had an Elizabethan treat for us. He went to the house to get it while we drooped dispiritedly on a little rustic bridge over a stream. We chose it because it had a bench, however uncomfortable, and was a little way from the damned hayfield. Roberts strode towards us exuberantly with tin cups and an earthenware jug which he crooked over his bent elbow, his forefinger hooked through the handle, and he poured us each a generous libation of his ancient mixture. I have lived for sixty years and have gagged down some nauseating medicines in my time, but to this day that concoction takes the prize. He called it "switchel," and its loathsomeness cannot be exaggerated. In the first place, it was lukewarm; and he told us proudly that it contained rum, lemon juice, molasses, and red pepper. I forget what else. In a short time, the stream below us was flowing with switchel, some of it thrown out and some of it thrown up. If the Elizabethans drank this to spur them on, I wonder that any farming was ever done.

Somehow we finished our haying and returned to Seawood, each bearing his or her own autographed Roberts book. The reward did not particularly alleviate the memory of our previous misery. In Roberts's house, a bookcase ran the length of the living room and contained *nothing* but copies of his own books. We thought he could have done better by his hardworking underpaid hayers. Hot baths did more for us than our payment for the grueling afternoon. Uncle Booth, highly amused by our dinner-table accounts of our hardships, said he was going to call Mrs. Roberts and Margery, Roberts's niece and long-suffering secretary, and suggest that they come over to his property to mend a stone wall that needed repairing and to clean out the finger system.

♦ ♦ ♦ ♦ ♦ ♦ ♦ ♦ ♦

EVEN WITH A HOUSE FULL OF COMPANY AT SEAWOOD, Uncle Booth in his older years worked every day in the Jacobean Room. He wrote as he had always done, with the same skill and scrupulous craftsmanship that is obvious in his earlier works. In the thirties, although he was downgraded by critics for being a conservative in an age of social, economic, and political change, he remained at the peak of popularity with his readers. He never allowed the changes in literary fashions to influence his presentations, generally feeling that the more things change, the more they remain the same. He steadfastly refused to allow the literary experts and critics to dictate his subject or delineation of characters. If his popularity had slipped with some, it did not seem to distress him; and he seemed more interested than ever in people, both living and dead. His mental powers increased, and along with them, his enthusiasm for art.

Seawood had thirty or more old portraits on its walls, mostly eighteenth- and nineteenth-century faces of the English school. When we visited in Maine, each night after dinner, Uncle Booth took Mig and me and any other guests on a guided tour of the portraits, each with its own shaded light making the paintings glow with soft color. Peering closely at the portraits through very thick glasses, he told the novices among us something new about a sitter every evening. He helped us really to see the warm paintings of the English school, pointing out the soft blush of a cheek and the sheen of damask and silk. I remember him vividly on these tours — slightly stooped, in dinner clothes, his expression revealing keen interest in both the portraits and us, as well as what we were learning — his ebullience, even in age, very evident as he did something he loved to do. On those tours, he had what one of his nieces called "his Kennebunkport look" — happy, rested, and serene. How patient he was with us.

He pointed out to us that the Seawood portraits showed much softer faces than those in the fifteenth- and sixteenth-century portraits in his Indianapolis house. The eighteenth and nineteenth centuries, he said, were gentler times. The expressions of the sitters reflected those conditions and contrasted with the wariness and hardness in the countenances from the earlier period. I would never have noticed this for myself. He took this ritual tour every night, and every night we learned something more. He wrote: ". . . bald indeed is the painting that does not reward an increasing intimacy. . . . there will be surprises not offered except to a continuing familiarity."[56]

IN THE TROUBLED YEARS BEFORE WORLD WAR II, UNCLE Booth had two great pleasures which were intertwined and which gave him joy rarely experienced by a person in his or her seventies. One was completion in 1939 of *Some Old Portraits,* a volume, illustrated with colored reproductions, about his portrait collection. He wrote the book out of his love for his pictures, not because it would sell. A market hardly existed in the thirties for books about the paintings from a private collection, and the nineteenth-century English school was then having a decline in popularity. I wonder how many of his admirers have read it or even heard of it? In this book, all of his talents and knowledge coalesce.

To Uncle Booth the mere acquisition and enjoyment of a painting as a work of art would have been a very limited experience. He always bought portraits of people about whom he could learn more — the social and political history of their times as well as the artistic climate. From his own research and the indefatigable work of Betty Trotter, he had learned not only the history but also the milieux and minutiae of the sitters' and artists' lives. He wove these various strands together, bringing to each page his own interpretation of what he saw in the face on the canvas. The sitters became his dear friends since he had studied them with more acumen than people usually study their own living best friends. He treated them all with kindliness and wrote in his preface, "Shall we not think of them fondly, we who are their continuation?"[57] As I studied *Some Old Portraits,* I realized that no man ever loved *things* more than he loved his portraits, so perhaps his great affection and encyclopedic knowledge of the sitters heightened his powers to portray them in prose. As a friend once wrote me about *Some Old Portraits,* Uncle Booth had "a sure touch as well as understanding and compassion, a feeling for words and great skill at contriving the fitting expression — and without strain or affectation."[58]

On a page in the front of my autographed copy is the statement: "This edition is limited to two hundred and forty-seven copies (of which two hundred and one are for sale)." How unfortunate that my two favorite Tarkington books, *Your Amiable Uncle* and *Some Old Portraits* — interestingly both nonfiction — are virtually unobtainable. The latter book reveals his real passion for art, and it was a passion second only to his writing. Of course, *Portraits* combines the two.

In the essays themselves, Uncle Booth demonstrated his involvement with the subject of each portrait and that person's history. In the preface, however, he showed his fascination with every aspect of the artistic process — from the time the sitter takes the pose until the artist finishes the painting and the viewer looks upon it. I believe it was the preface as much as the book itself which prompted Erwin Panofsky to rate *Some Old Portraits* as a unique work — high praise from a man so famous in the history-of-art world. He felt that an art historian could not have written it, " 'a book that compels the painter to tell us more about human nature than he reveals in the picture, and compels the sitter to tell us more about human nature than he revealed to the painter.' "[59]

In the preface, with empathy and understanding, Uncle Booth put himself into the thoughts and emotions of the three people involved in a portrait — the painter, the beholder, and the subject. In the words of the painter: " 'While I'm working I never let a thought of anybody's applause or displeasure affect one stroke of my brush; nevertheless, in the far back of my mind I'm aware all the time of an audience I'm trying to reach. . . . an ideal audience that will understand me and see what I believe I'm expressing. Such an audience, I know, is only an artist's gossamer dream. . . . The best actual audience a painter can hope for is one that will be fair enough to suspend judgment until it has first found out what he's trying to do; then is competent enough to discover how well he does it; and finally is so all-wise as to know whether or not it's worth doing.' "[60]

As the beholder, Uncle Booth warned about being swayed by pronouncements of "Authorities — art historians, art philosophers, scholars, critics, esthetes, connoisseurs, and the painters themselves": "Our enthusiasm and our disapprovals are our own; and, whether we lose or gain by them, so long as we preserve them from becoming mere echoes we are entitled to them. . . . Egoistic instinct is subtle and glamorous: it can even mistake itself for authoritative judgment upon works of art; but if we avoid being carried away by its eloquence we needn't share in the error. That is, by making ourselves a little hard-headed we can escape the confusion of mind that damns an ostrich for not being a giraffe."[61]

Concerning the subject, Uncle Booth wrote: " . . . shall we not be as interested in the subject of a picture as is the painter himself? If he sees a human being as so much 'still life' . . . we too can try to see the subject . . . as so much 'still life' . . . but if the painter is interested in the human qualities of his subject . . . we do [him] little justice if we refuse to see what he has felt and seen and done. . . . When art is the illuminating interpreter of a life, painting it memorably, we're given a great portrait." Uncle Booth commented upon "the love of oldness" in portraits: "It is a tenderness toward what was made and used and sometimes loved by men and women who can make and use and love no more. This love of oldness, moreover,

Top: *Portraits in the Indianapolis house flank the Spanish campaign desk before which Susanah Jameson and Francis Mayberry were married in 1944.* Above left: *Dobson's true portrait of young John Milton re-* vealed to Tarkington's ophthalmologist that the poet was going blind. Above right: *Lely's Nell Gwyn shows "a joking little woman who threw her clothes on anyhow."*

carries the fond perception of our kinship with the life and art that preceded our own brief living. . . . [It] isn't . . . an 'escape into the past'; we bring old enrichments into our present." He warned, however, that "though there is no prohibition that can prevent us from loving oldness for its own sake, our eyes serve us hazily when they confuse oldness with art."[62]

And this is the way Uncle Booth viewed his own paintings: "We shall think of the portrait, so far as we are able, as a work of art; we shall think of it as a bit of history, as a relic, and as a human thing in its own age and in ours. We shall indulge ourselves with thoughts concerning whatever concerned the painter, the picture and the sitter; we shall indulge ourselves in reflections stimulated within us by such thoughts. In brief, from the picture we shall get everything, of every kind, that we know how to get."[63]

Uncle Booth's great enthusiasm for his pictures was an essential and integral part of his later years. No book of reminiscences about him would be complete without a look at a few of the lovingly written essays in *Some Old Portraits*.

He wrote of Sir Peter Lely's portrait of Nell Gwyn, a mistress of Charles II:

> *Blurred a little, she yet glances from this old oval – Nell Gwyn, a joking little woman who threw on her clothes anyhow, yet so that they became her, a daughter of Nature and the Comic Muse, an inspired stage farceuse, a king's favorite without greed or ambition – a slum child who danced up out of darkness into the light of history, danced and laughed for a moment in the august glow, then dropped down again, young, into the darkness.*[64]

Who else could have written more compassionately and understandingly of Sir Joshua Reynolds?

> *He bought "Old Masters" and when at the last of his life, after his many years of deafness, he was blind, too, he stood and stood before these pictures, feeling their surfaces delicately with his hand, still studying them perceptively and fondly. In that complete isolation from everything else – old, hearing nothing with his ears, seeing nothing with his eyes – he still had this vital companionship. . . . He was a painter.*[65]

What I have said about the background and exquisite writing in this book is nowhere more vividly illustrated than in Uncle Booth's essay about Mary Stuart, Princess of Orange, by Sir Peter Lely:

> *Her greatest sorrows were over when she sat to Lely; but
> there is a trace of them. She was in her twenties, when months
> still can seem long, and years had passed since those heaviest
> griefs of hers; yet one of the undercurrents of her look is a
> certain wariness, the on-guard expression that even youth may
> have when it has already learned that any terrible thing may
> happen at any time. . . .*
>
> *She had loved her husband . . . and his death came at a
> dreadful time for her. Her father, whom she adored, had been
> beheaded by his own people the year before. . . . she alone of
> the dispersed and ruined family held any power. . . . and her
> baby was born during the first agony of her widowhood. . . .*
>
> *She's wary, yet couldn't be frightened – a proud, generous,
> dauntless, loyal, little-headed Stuart Princess no wiser than the
> others of the unwise race of which she is the lovely
> incarnation.*[66]

Sometimes the portrait by William Dobson of the young John
Milton was at Seawood. Dr. William Wilmer, the eminent ophthalmologist who took care of Uncle Booth during his siege of critical
eye trouble, was once at the Tarkingtons'; and when he looked
closely at Milton's portrait, he said, "I can tell that he's going blind."
William Dobson had painted truly, indeed. Maybe Uncle Booth became interested in the painting in the first place because of his own
eye problems. He wrote of this painting, ". . . no one can stand before this portrait, even without the knowledge that John Milton is
there, and not say, 'Here is a great man!' "[67]

My own favorite painting was of Augusta Montagu by Gilbert
Stuart, and it hung over the mantel in the living room. In her childhood she had been the victim of a terrifying scandal, but Stuart
painted her

> *as gay and as lightly touched as if he'd painted a momentary
> poise of blowing petals. . . .*
>
> *She wasn't beautiful; she wasn't pretty; but she had blue
> eyes, tawny hair and the ineffable coatings of youth that bedeck
> all healthy human beings, for a little while, as they pass through
> their one fancy-dress party of being young.*
>
> *Gilbert Stuart saw the wonder of it – that this volatile romp
> of a girl danced out of so dreadful a background – and it was his
> delight to paint her, tenderly, as wholly unshadowed by what lay
> behind her. . . . and when, after laughing, she had a little reverie
> about sweethearts and the future, he painted her as quickly as
> he could. . . .*
>
> *Every old painter has a day when he looks back and says to
> himself, "Of course I've learned a great deal since then – but ah,
> I did do a lovely thing* that *time!"*[68]

I believe I would give almost anything to have Augusta over *my* mantel. This achingly lovely portrait seems to embody all of my memories of those happy times. One had only to glance up from one of the couches that flanked the fireplace to see the ribbons of her bonnet fluttering in the breeze and her dreaming expression. I hope all the paintings have found happy homes and are loved as much as they were when I knew them — especially Augusta.

◆ ◆ ◆ ◆ ◆ ◆ ◆ ◆ ◆

UNCLE BOOTH'S SECOND GREAT JOY WAS HIS FRIENDSHIP with German-born Erwin Panofsky. In 1938 in Kennebunkport through mutual friends, he had met and found instant rapport with and love for Dr. and Mrs. Panofsky. Panofsky, a matchless art historian, teacher, and author, was then completing a book on the Renaissance. Richard Ludwig, editor of *Dr. Panofsky and Mr. Tarkington: An Exchange of Letters, 1938 –* 1946, quotes John Coolidge, former director of Harvard's Fogg Museum of Art, who described being with Panofsky as " 'living next door to a lighthouse. Objectively you watched the beam revolve until suddenly you yourself were drenched by his ebullience, by his crackling perceptions, by his overwhelming, unaccountable kindness.' "[69]

In 1931 at age forty-six, Panofsky was internationally famous, on leave from Hamburg University, and teaching as a visiting professor at New York University. Two years later he was fired from the Hamburg University in Hitler's purge. Their being in America saved the Panofsky family from a dire fate. This outstanding scholar later was invited to be a permanent member of the Institute for Advanced Study in its School of Humanistic Studies at Princeton, New Jersey.

The Panofskys were on vacation from Princeton when they met the Tarkingtons; the couples were not strangers from the moment they met. The two men formed an immediate and rare friendship: Panofsky, fifty-three, Jewish, a scholar, European to the core; and Tarkington, in his seventies, gentile, a writer, a midwestern American. Although disparate in age and background, their talents were complementary — both were writers as well as art connoisseurs. Their friendship was further cemented by their catholicity of interests and enthusiasm for life. These elements seemed to dovetail as if designed by a benign Providence. In a letter dated September 23, 1943, to Uncle Booth, Dr. Panofsky wrote: "I am quite serious in saying that I consider your friendship one of the greatest favors Fate has bestowed upon me. Meeting you is meeting a whole world (much of which was entirely new to me) and a whole period of history."[70]

I did not know that a book of their letters existed until I was telephoning Alexander Wainright of the Princeton University Library on another matter. He told me about it and kindly sent me a complimentary copy. Richard Ludwig, who compiled the letters, says in the preface that the correspondence is a "remarkable collection . . . for the light it throws on private lives during wartime." He adds, 'Generosity of spirit is in every page. . . . In spite of failing eyesight, he [Uncle Booth] answered Panofsky's handwritten letters with a shaky but determined pen. . . . The salutations never varied: Dear Dr. Panofsky, Dear Mr. Tarkington. *Dulce et decorum est.*"[71]

To me the letters reveal a *politesse du coeur* and an old world courtesy sadly lacking in our day of area codes and numbered accounts. And they certainly reveal their authors' wide range of interests. The correspondents discussed their hopes for an effective United Nations, hopes that even then were tinged with doubt because they both realized that nations would probably be unwilling to yield sovereignty to any world authority. They wrote with great apprehension about the catastrophic possibilities implicit in splitting the atom — and this before August 1945. And the two men gladly aided each other in their respective careers. Uncle Booth must have given Dr. Panofsky some helpful criticism on a book he was writing about Dürer. On September 23, 1943, he thanked Uncle Booth for the suggested rearrangement of material, "Of course, you looked upon my book with an especially benevolent eye; but even so I feel very much elated."[72]

To provide background for a Tarkington-Panofsky exchange of letters which had humor at its core, I must introduce Mr. Rumbin and his prototype. Uncle Booth wrote the Rumbin stories in the thirties and early forties for the *Saturday Evening Post,* and they were later collected into the book *Rumbin Galleries.* Both Abris and David Silberman of New York, Uncle Booth's chief art dealers, were models for Mr. Rumbin, but mainly David because he spoke colorful broken English which was faithfully copied in the book's dialogue. Uncle Booth had learned much from firsthand experience in the art world through buying pictures from the Silbermans. Some of those experiences he treated in a humorous way in his writing.

In the stories Mr. Rumbin is the owner of an art gallery in New York and always financially embarrassed. Uncle Booth described him as having "a wide silhouette," being "a middle-aged active fat man with a glowing eye," and speaking in "a foreign accent of elusive origin."[73] A man of unassailable ego and never above chicanery, Mr. Rumbin believes that his knowledge on all matters pertaining to art is encyclopedic. Uncle Booth's pleasure was to fondly put down his creation. Mr. Rumbin, though, has surprising buoyancy, bobbing up like a cork and often managing to turn his mistakes to his own advantage. The gallery owner has a predilection for puffing up self-importantly at the very moment he is displaying inadequate knowledge of his field. This attitude inspired Uncle Booth to request help from Dr. Panofsky in teaching Mr. Rumbin a lesson. Dr. Panofsky was at that time writing *The Abbey Church of St. Denis and Its Art Treasures.*

Concerning the episode, Ludwig writes in *Dr. Panofsky and Mr. Tarkington,* "On October 3 [1943] Betty Trotter had written to Dr. Panofsky to say 'Mr. T. is writing a Rumbin story' and needs help." She discussed Uncle Booth's need at length and wrote that Mr. Rumbin, showing off as usual, had destroyed the reputation of an *objet d'art* by saying it was not authentic. Mr. Tarkington, she said, wanted this *objet* to be very old and very rare, one of Abbé Suger's from St. Denis, and he wondered if his friend could tell him what "'the *objet* could might plausibly be.'" She added that Mr. Tarkington would like "' . . . its being brought out, to complete Mr. Rumbin's discomfiture, that your translation describes the *objet*.'"

Dr. Panofsky suggested "the gondola of St. Eloy, a boat or 'navette' (employed for holding the grains of incense) carved from prase or jade, and decorated with cloisonné enamel, formerly in the treasury of the abbey church."[74] The gondola appears in the story "Mr. Rumbin's Blessed Misfortune" in the *Saturday Evening Post* dated May 19, 1945. Uncle Booth "gave full credit to Panofsky for his assistance" and introduced him into the story as "a character named Professor Schnöder as the authority on Suger."[75]

On another occasion my uncle mixed humor with whimsy when he wrote a thank-you letter to the Panofskys for a birthday present. They had sent him a walking stick with an ivory handle that had belonged to an old Cape Cod ship's captain, and he was delighted with the gift. He replied on August 1, 1940, writing as if the original owner — "Master of a ship, no less" — had left his cane in the hall and was "now in the living-room, carrying his top-hat and gloves with him, in high stateliness, as he talks of Chinese Seas, Sumatra, Callao, and Bombay curries, and nibbles cake and tosses down his glass of wine." Uncle Booth added, "Never *was* there a more

Although from different worlds, Booth Tarkington and Dr. Erwin Panofsky formed an immediate and rare friendship. Above: Tarkington — in his seventies, gentile, a professional writer, and midwestern American. Left: Panofsky — in his fifties, Jewish, a scholar, and European to the core.

eloquent cane. . . . Such kindness helps one to be calm under the indignity of enlarging numbers."[76]

Ludwig says that the letters show a "generosity of spirit," and it is nowhere more evident than in the letter Uncle Booth wrote on November 5, 1944, to Dr. Panofsky. He and his wife were distressed by the signs of anti-Semitism in America in World War II. The letter was a lengthy one, and it was filled with reassurance:

Dear Dr. Panofsky:

"I write in haste" because of your saying that you and Mrs. Panofsky are distressed by an antisemitic ebullition. Take my word for it: you can laugh at it. Nothing of that sort can do you the slightest harm unless you let it make you apprehensive or hurt your feelings. Antisemitism in this country is the most futile of gestures and can't be more. Naturally, after what happened in Germany, I know how such a gesture would loom large in your minds, disturbing your imaginations; but don't waste anxiety on such impotences as mere nose-thumbing which is all the stuff amounts to. . . .

I've been of an "outcast-race" myself at times – enough to make me incredulously half resentful, half-amused. The manifestations were "Eastern," because I came from the Midwest – Indiana in particular – and am a Hoosier. "We never think of you as from Indiana" was said to me consolingly more than once in my youth. . . .

"Gangs" in cities don't like people who differ in appearance or customs or heritage from themselves. In Boston there's been Jew-baiting by hoodlums. In Indianapolis there have been gang fights between Irish and Negroes. In many smaller towns, South side fights North side, etc. Chinamen have been stoned for sport, Jewish boys joining in. Hoodlumism is hoodlumism; it isn't antisemitism.

He summed up that anyone could run into " 'social embarrass-ments'; but they would be petty." He said he had once overheard two ladies refuse to sit at his table because he pronounced "watuh" and "buttah" as " 'wat-*tur*' " and " 'but-*tur*,' " adding that there is always someone in the world to whom someone else objects. "In Germany the objectee couldn't laugh at the objector. Here he can and does."[77]

From Princeton on November 11, 1944, Dr. Panofsky answered:

Dear Mr. Tarkington:

I can hardly tell you how touched we both are by your kindness in spending so much time, labor and thought on

assuaging what must have struck you as unnecessary
misgivings. . . .
    Concerning the question of antisemitism, I am convinced . . .
that you are perfectly right in diagnosing it, in its present form,
as something very different from its European manifestations
– hoodlumism on the one hand and snobbery on the other. . . . I
am, personally, rather in favor of the "snobbish" form of
discrimination; for as long as it remains snobbish, it is less likely
to merge with the hoodlumish variety, and it is only the fusion of
these two, sanctioned by a sort of philosophy, which transforms
discrimination and sporadic outbreaks of violence into
organized persecution.[78]

Some of these letters are more than ten pages long. The friends exchanged books, letters, and affection. Making a cherished new friend when one is in one's mid-seventies is a favor given only to a chosen few; and more than that, it implies a talent for love. I never had the privilege of meeting Dr. Panofsky (although I must have *nearly* met him during my Maine visits from 1938 to 1942), but I hold his memory dear and would have loved overhearing one of the conversations between him and my uncle.

He wrote a tribute to Uncle Booth in March 1946, and this was before Uncle Booth's death:

It will never be known how many people are indebted to his
generosity in financial matters; but no less numerous must be
those who are indebted to his generosity in matters of the spirit.
It is, in general, sadly true that illness and age make men
self-centered. Booth Tarkington, who has gone through many an
illness and is now nearly seventy-seven, appears to be more
rather than less concerned about his fellow-beings. I know of
men and women who might not have survived a crisis of
suspense and despair had not Booth Tarkington fortified them
with the strength of his understanding and sympathy.[79]

♦ ♦ ♦ ♦ ♦ ♦ ♦ ♦ ♦

MOST OF MY OWN CORRESPONDENCE WITH UNCLE BOOTH was written when I was at Smith College in Massachusetts. During those years he wrote me so often that I wondered when he had time to write his books. No college freshman ever took herself more seriously than I. Uncle Booth, being the perfect confidant, received all my complaints; and as my aunt said once, "You can't keep Uncle

Booth answered." He used to return a letter to me the day he received mine, always in longhand on a bright yellow-orangish thick paper, almost cardboard, that helped him see a little better. His prodigious correspondence ranged from the reassuring letter in 1944 to Dr. Panofsky about anti-Semitism to the consoling and gently preceptorial letters in 1939 to me about the problems of a bemused college freshman away from home for the first time.

Because I was in New England where skiing, at least in the movies, looked exciting, I elected it as my freshman sport. I had visions of myself gliding effortlessly down the mountains, escorted of course by a bronzed and handsome young man. Our ski tracks would make figure eights as we casually swooped down the slopes. This daydream was abruptly terminated. When I was on skis, I could not even learn how to stop once I had started down a hill, however small. In fact, I had to fall down if I wanted to stop. I wrote Uncle Booth sadly about my difficulties, and he replied:

> *How true what you say of sports. They really oughtn't to be called that, and if they were known instead as hardships – which is what they really are – this world (as people somewhat too frequently say) would be a better place. I learned early to participate in all outdoor pastimes visually. In that manner I enjoyed entering into them heart and soul even when they were of the roughest nature and required the highest quality of fortitude. I fear you may think I'm setting myself up as a model, but the modest truth is that I'm only offering experience as suggestive. On the Scrub at Purdue I was placed opposite a Varsity guard, formerly an ironworker, who had unfortunately killed his best friend in football practice the year before. I found it always best just to watch him when his duties required him to pass me by. I suppose the illusion of pleasure obtained from skiing is founded in the sensation of sliding. I believe that no animal except the human deceives itself in this manner . . . chill and lack of safety and a momentary proof that Sir Isaac Newton was right seem to be the reward of the ski-ist – obtained by long and sometimes anguished labor.*[80]

In addition to athletic failures, my freshman year also had academic hardships which were quite a blow to my pride. Full of self-confidence in my scholastic abilities, I truly thought there had been some mistake then I saw a *D* in history on my grade card, but a visit to the history professor confirmed the sad truth. Naturally I did not think I should have received such an ignominious grade, but there it was; and someone had to soften the blow at home. I wrote confidently to Uncle Booth hoping that he could fix everything up for me. When my own children brought home grades that were less than I had expected from them, I used to remember his answer to me:

> *I'll do what I can about your "D"... I'll ask your mother to let me have the chart when it arrives so that I can delicately remove it and substitute a graceful "A" before your father is told that news has come. Nothing is simpler. I realize how easily these mistakes occur; in large institutions of learning the clerkly error hovers ever, because of the vast quantity of reports to be sent out, because of lapses of mind on the part of transcribers, because of vaguenesses in the records and estimates of groping professors.... I received a first group in Astronomy in my Junior year at Princeton, delighting my father and mother who hadn't known that I was working in that field at all; and as I hadn't been and the praise should all have gone to some other, whose identity I lightheartedly never sought to discover, I had to leave home every evening of the ensuing summer before the stars came out.*[81]

I wrote to him about Ann's and my disappointment and anger when we had been turned down at the last minute by two gentlemen we had invited to a dance. In the parlance of the day, we had been "stood up." Uncle Booth sent lighthearted words of wisdom, which were not at the time particularly appreciated, I am afraid. Our disappointment at being turned down by the boys we thought we had favored by our invitations was increased by our fury at their excuses. One of them had to play in a golf tournament; the other one had polo practice. Or so they said. Uncle Booth wrote, and with great amusement I am sure:

> *Suppose they had said they couldn't come because of a sheep shearing contest and a checkers tournament. Would that make the pain any easier? Certainly not. They give the best excuses for absence an honorable young man can find anywhere — golf and polo. In my youth when we couldn't (or felt indisposed to) keep an engagement we* always *said we were sick. Golf and polo are a lot more serious reasons than sickness and ought to satisfy any waiting lady. We didn't have golf or polo at our disposal or we'd have been more popular; the girls would have understood better and admired us more because there's something feeble about being sick even when it's true. No modern young man, unable to afford car fare or gas and tires would say that sickness detains him; he'd say he had to break a hunter.... Of course, the line of conduct is always the same,*

*generation after generation. When the absentee does appear, if
he does, in his own good time, the lady is so brightly friendly, in
a lightly amused way, that he thinks someone else did
arrive – maybe several – when he didn't. Sometimes it puts him
in his place, almost – for a little while. . . .*

*I hope you retain your powers of perspective in affairs of
the imagination – perhaps I should say affairs of the heart.
Perhaps though, the perspective doesn't arrive until
later – maybe as much as two or three affairs later, sometimes
seven or eight. Of course, if you begin to suffer from the Grand
Passion of your whole life, that's all different; but how can you
tell whether it is or not; one test is supposed to be getting at what
you'd really feel about him if he had crossed eyes and a mobile
adams apple and you were his next door neighbor's
grandmother. Applying this carefully, slowly, conscientiously and
examiningly has helped one or two cases during the last three
centuries. Until after Henry VIII there wasn't any help at all.*[82]

DURING MY COLLEGE YEARS, MY SELF-ABSORPTION WAS
so complete that I gave hardly a thought to my brother and sister at
home, beyond picturing them in a state of suspended animation,
waving at me on the station platform as I left and still waving as my
train pulled in for vacations. It never occurred to me that anything
would happen to them while I was away. But if Florence and Johnny
were shadowy figures to me, their lives both exterior and interior,
fascinated Uncle Booth. My sister was nine when I went to college
and never had talked much about herself to me or to Johnny, probably because we did not listen to her when she did. But with Uncle
Booth, she became an animated dinner partner. He, the best of
storytellers, was also the best of listeners, and she delighted him. He
teased her gently because her third-grade teacher had written on
her report card, "Florence is a leader in her own quiet way." He
always referred to her as the Divine Flora and had her sit next to
him at dinner:

*The Divine Flora dined with us last night, and looking
brilliantly eloquent, though small-voiced, indicated to me that
she felt she had by no means disgraced herself in a final test in
social studies endured some hours before. She also shed lights
on Egypt which she is now studying. She declined to agree on
my pronunciations such as Spinx and Spinkusses. . . . Last month
she was absorbed in Babylon, and her parting words to me were*

> *gently chiding. I was mistaken in believing that the Babylonians*
> *hanged all the gardeners; it was the gardens that hung.*[83]

I realize now that if I had really studied his letters about the younger members of my family, I would have known much more about them than if I had stayed at home.

It is laboring the obvious to add that the adolescent boy, especially if he were in love or in trouble, was always a source of pure delight to Uncle Booth. His remarks about the true motives of boys will make mothers of little girls feel tremblingly protective. His views confirm what mothers have suspected all along:

> *I am told that Fenton and Johnny [my cousin and brother]*
> *are being trained to cut-in and often do it on the wrong party;*
> *after which they show symptoms of pride and*
> *self-congratulation. To us this doesn't seem to indicate that they*
> *do it ignorantly; no, our conclusion is that they do it with an*
> *inner purpose. . . . When a boy cuts in, his feelings are almost*
> *wholly egoistic. "I'll break that up. Get out of here, you sap."*
> *Thoughts about the girl's preference don't happen once in a*
> *thousand times, and as for the cut-off boy, the cutter-in hopes*
> *he's sore. I think this is still true. I doubt if the animals have*
> *changed much since I was one of them – or since the glacial age*
> *for that matter.*
>
> *Young Marmie Home's mother told your Aunt Susanah that*
> *Fenton took Marmie to a party, having previously swelled up to*
> *flower-sending for the first time in his life. He sent one gardenia*
> *and four leaves. On the way home, fearing that there might be*
> *some appearance of inadequacy, he said to the little girl, "I*
> *believe that is the lousiest corsage I ever sent. I'm going to*
> *remove my patronage from that florist shop."*[84]

For adolescents, parents can be a trial almost too great to be borne; and my brother, when he was twelve and in love, found his naturally inquisitive family an insupportable burden. He announced to his baffled mother and father that he was going to lead his own life, and he achieved quite a remarkable success. Uncle Booth watched his efforts to become an invisible man with fascinated respect and admiration. In 1940 when I was a sophomore at Smith, he wrote to me about it:

> *At the age of three Johnny obtained that whole control over*
> *voice and features necessary to one who contemplates living*
> *with his family on terms of chronic dissimulation. In this art he*
> *has become a master, the peer of whom is not revealed to me by*
> *the utmost stress I can put into my research among youthful*
> *memories. There is much for us all to learn of him. We don't*

understand him much better than the Court at Elsinore
understood Hamlet, though thinking of Johnny as Hamlet doesn't
seem quite right, more like Calvin Coolidge with a strong touch
of Romeo. I have long had the feeling that Johnny doesn't live
on the surface and is, indeed, seldom to be found there. He has,
of course, developed a perfect technique to meet his parents'
solicitude, equipped his ears with automatic stoppers.[85]

The more Uncle Booth found out about Johnny's love life, the more delighted he was. The object of Johnny's affections was a girl who had made the football team when he could not. Uncle Booth's penchant for teasing reached new heights when the young lady in question threw notes tied to stones through the bedroom window when Johnny was sick with the measles. He really caught the brunt of Uncle Booth's raillery, and the result was that he never told *anybody anything again.* "Calvin Coolidge with a strong touch of Romeo" indeed.

Uncle Booth, naturally enough, enjoyed his great-nieces and great-nephews somewhat more than their harried parents did: with laughter and love, he observed the trials and triumphs of our growing up. He sympathized with both the grown-ups and the children. He understood and completely enjoyed the despair of the parents as well as the determination of his great-nephews to get themselves into trouble just as easily as their fathers had done. He wrote me about one incident of delinquency which gave him intense pleasure:

Last evening your parents seemed distracted and Johnny
was not present. Your father had instinctively refused to let him
go to Brown County for Easter vacation with fifteen untutored
boys. (Of course, Johnny did *go.) Nature is interesting but queer;*
your Pa was never let go any *place and made some fusses*
about that. Nowadays – aware that he might have drowned or
fallen from a cliff if he had been allowed to run free, he's afraid
to let his children do anything. So they have to screech him into
it. Why does he worry? I'm afraid its because he sets quite a
value on his three young – for obscure reasons best known to
himself. Mysterious.[86]

Saying "no" was a matter of principle with my father, so we usually did not pay much attention to his automatic objections; but his instinct was right about the trip to southern Indiana's Brown County. The boys, several of whom were known to every cow and grasshopper for miles around, thought up some new amusements — housebreaking, destruction, and vandalism. When the terrible truth was discovered, everybody went to considerable effort to keep the knowledge of the crimes from Uncle Booth. They should

Upper left: *Lt. John Jameson, Jr., (Johnny) shortly after receiving his commission at seventeen — "an Officer and a Gentleman."* Upper right: *Susanah Jameson (Susie) in 1942 when she graduated from Smith College.* Left: *Florence Jameson ("the Divine Flora") at fifteen — the year of her Grand Passion.* Below: *John Jameson at about the time his offspring, Johnny, Susie, and "the Divine Flora," were involved in an intense correspondence with their amiable uncle.*

have known better. He wrote to me about the boys before anyone else did.

> *We dined with your family last night and when Flora*
> *opened the door for us, I noted, but couldn't define at once her*
> *expression. She had that* look – *worn only by little sisters when*
> *their big brothers are in serious trouble. It gave us all a mighty*
> *interesting evening. Fenton and Johnny were worth a whole lot*
> *of covert looking at! A perfect triumph for your father after the*
> *fight he put up to forbid Johnny's going to Brown County, but he*
> *didn't seem to appreciate his moral advantage, maybe because*
> *of the cost of damages. Flora was a study all evening – the*
> *gravity of little sister, loyal, but knows of terrible goings on*
> *under the social surface.*
>
> *From the side table where banqueted Miss Flora and*
> *Johnny and Fenton, there came not any murmur of*
> *conversation. I should've known then that something awful had*
> *been going on, but didn't "get" things until we returned to the*
> *living room where I couldn't help stirring up the waters. Fenton*
> *attempted spotty bits of jaunty self-exculpation, but Johnny,*
> *always in character, said never a word.*[87]

On October 3, 1944, Uncle Booth wrote another letter about my younger brother — this to my father — after Johnny, having left high school in his junior year, had received his Air Force commission as a navigator on one of the B-17 bombers which daily and nightly were bombing Germany in great numbers in World War II:

> *I expect we're about as proud of J.T.J.Jr. as you are . . . Lt!*
> *Well, he's an Officer and Gentleman, in the service of his*
> *country in time of war, and I don't know how anybody in the*
> *world can be anything greater than that. At his age, just out of*
> *boyhood, he's gone as high as any man can. General*
> *Eisenhower has superior rank; but that's a technical*
> *difference. . . .*
>
> *It's not been easy. The sharpest kind of trial's been*
> *involved – trial of soul and mind and body – and he's out on top,*
> *ready to ride the skies for the Great Republic! We're all proud to*
> *be kin to him!*[88]

After his plane had been shot up over Germany and had limped back to England, vulnerable, alone, and at greatly reduced speed, Johnny wrote only to Uncle Booth about it. It goes without saying that Uncle Booth kept the confidence — as Johnny, of course, knew he would.

◆ ◆ ◆ ◆ ◆ ◆ ◆ ◆ ◆

WHEN UNCLE BOOTH WAS IN INDIANAPOLIS, HE KNEW ALL about our private lives by watching how we looked and acted; and when he was in Maine, he still knew because we all informed on each other with regularity and delight. He, of course, strongly urged us to take these somewhat low measures, but we never felt that we were being underhanded. I think we must have tacitly agreed that he had a kind of avuncular immunity; certainly we never considered playing private eye for anyone else.

I like to think that our motives were at least partly benevolent. We wanted to entertain him, and his letters back to us always indicated that we had, probably much more than we knew. His answers caused both the informer and the one informed upon to feel a happy glow of self-importance, and, of course, insured a steady flow of information for him. There were certain pitfalls, though, for the over-enthusiastic informer.

In the summer of 1941, I was reporting to him all the details I knew about my sister's summer romance. She was fifteen years old and having her first experience with a Grand Passion. I made my initial mistake when I told him that the two principals had exchanged identification bracelets. His answer was immediate and joyful:

> *In my own don't-tell-papa days if me and my friends could have found a little boy that wore a bracelet he'd received from a fair hand, we'd have had hours and days and weeks of good wholesome sadistic happiness and tremendous activity. There'd have been not one waking hour of loneliness for either of 'em; songs would have been composed and sung and sung and sung. Poems, slogans and catch-words would have sounded and resounded up and down Pennsylvania, Meridian and Delaware Streets until adult sufferings brought intervention. The thought brings me the severest nostalgia, especially on such a birthday as at the moment assails me! What perplexes me most is your father's giving his assent to everything. I've always thought him a man of quite strong prejudices. It's hard to imagine him as peacefully getting the young man out at night and quietly going up to bed with his candle.*
>
> *Sixty years ago the little girl's family always put us out at mealtimes. They didn't tell us to go—just rang the dinner bell till we got the idea and left. Sometimes we'd hear a middle-aged voice calling: "Isn't he gone yet? Ring it again, Lobelia!"*[89]

In the next mail, I received another letter from Uncle Booth. I had got in over my head this time:

Please secure for me the total correspondence in this case. I
should like to publish it with only a slight editing. Do not let any
sisterly or even human scruples stand in your way. Remember,
within a matter of weeks the principals won't even know what it
was all about. (How fitful and flitterbird is the school-age heart!)
I remember a dreadful period in my own experience when I was
like that (after a summer at Maxinkuckee) through the whole
month *of September, an object of commiseration by everybody*
in our neighborhood.[90]

Florence had always been a biddable child, eager to please. I
started my campaign to get the letters with considerable optimism.
Ignoring any pangs of conscience, I began to mention the letters in
conversations. "I bet Uncle Booth would just love to see your letters.
He certainly would appreciate it if you'd send them to him," I would
say brightly. "He might even send you a present he'd be so glad."
This infantile approach might have worked a few years earlier, but
not any more! She never even heard me. Smiling vaguely, she
wandered away. And all the time Uncle Booth was sending me
urgent letters like this one:

I cannot but feel you haven't gone about this correspon-
dence with energy and ingenuity. For instance, I don't believe
you've tried so simple a device as "Oh-look-at-that-Giant-
across-the street," and when she looks, grab the letters and run.
It seems to me that a more active mind would long since have
thought of this.[91]

I was in a terrible spot. I could not nerve myself up to outright
theft, but everything else I had tried had ended in failure because
she seemed dreamily unaware that I even wanted the letters. When
she was at home, which was not often, she was in another world,
one that was impenetrable to my suggestions. Finally I took a mean
and bullying advantage of her bemused condition. Speaking loudly
and slowly, I told her she had to let me send those letters to Uncle
Booth. I promised that I would not read them, that she would get
them back, and that the young man would never know about it.
"Well, all right," she said mildly. "You don't have to yell at me."
Uncle Booth was overjoyed and answered immediately after
receiving the package of letters:

So far my examination of the files has revealed only the
usual stigmata, so much so, that when I read the mss. at the
lunch table your Aunt Susanah would not believe in the
genuineness of the missives, but insisted that I had written them

myself, as material for a new study of adolescence. However, though incredible to the inexperienced, the symptoms include all the registered phenomena. Strongly *marked is the delusion that the subject is writing* letters *whereas he, of course, mistakes the merely autobiographical for the epistolary and, in addition, records only what he feels most creditable to himself. Note the items of his adventurous peeking into a saloon maybe going to be raided by the State Police, (proprietors often spread such rumors among their most impecunious visitors who are of the credulous ages). Note, too, his dark account of being interviewed by the police about firecrackers – how he seeks to put about himself the haunting aura of danger. Also of persecution. Observe symptoms of stuttering when he writes of his vilely spiteful parents – how they un-understand him so viciously that he almost decided to end-it-all and get the hell out of there. All of this is typical – I might say pricelessly so – and the subject's ruthless "Old Codger" and "Old Lady," no doubt totteringly into their forties, probably ought to remember when* they *were 13 to 16 and wanted automobiles, lunch passes and other Rights of the Underprivileged.*

Anyhow this whole household enjoyed every word and gratitude to you is extreme. Now if we could only get hold of Flora's own autobiographical sketches – but I suppose that's too much to hope, and your Aunt Susanah would insist I could write them myself. Not quite – there are some modern touches I wouldn't be up to.[92]

It was bad enough that I had taken advantage of Florence's lovelorn condition. Worse still was my shameless delight when I read that *I*, not Florence, was to be rewarded for it. His letter ended, "So pleased was I with your strong arm work that I climbed the rope into the attic, and when I'd combed off my cobwebs, there were you, all fixed to receive six Hitchcock chairs, four yellow ones for the sides and two black for the foot and head of your table." (I have done all the work on this book, sitting in one of the Hitchcocks.)

◆ ◆ ◆ ◆ ◆ ◆ ◆ ◆ ◆

I HAVE LOOKED THROUGH THE LETTERS UNCLE BOOTH wrote to Florence and discovered that *she* sent *him* reports in 1943 when I had a Grand Passion of my own, this after my college years. She says she cannot remember what *she* told *him*, but this is what he answered:

> *Does your father sit on the top step* every evening *listening to Susanah propose to Lt. Mayberry? Please get him to tell you everything they say to each other. I think you can expect him to accept the invitation pretty soon now.*
>
> *If she and her Lt., as you say, don't talk about anything when you are with them, why not have a book ready to read aloud to them? Since he is about to leave Camp Atterbury, isn't it your duty to cheer them up and get them to talking again? It would be polite, wouldn't it, to make a list of subjects from the Encyclopedia so as to be entertaining and instructive when he comes on his visits? In this way you can become a useful sister improving everything. I do hope you will follow this suggestion. You are already a popular girl, but opportunities to grow even more so oughn't to be neglected.*[93]

(My father really did listen!) Lt. Francis T. Mayberry soon accepted my proposal, and we were married in January 1944.

Frank was sent to the European Theater of Operations six weeks after we had been married and came home in the early autumn of 1945 — *the most* exciting thing that ever happened to me! A couple of nights later we went to the Tarkingtons. Frank had told me a little bit of a story he could not wait to tell Uncle Booth.

After VE Day Frank had been sent to Paris to await transport to the United States. He was billeted in or near a red-light district and nearby was a bar frequented by transient soldiers. The prostitutes were steady customers, too, never soliciting, I had been told, but coming in "after work" for a drink or two. *Sotto voce* Frank began to talk to Uncle Booth. I was too far away to hear much, but I eavesdropped as much as I could. The story caused Uncle Booth to have near convulsions of laughter. (As Frank went on, Uncle Booth began to rock back and forth, as he must have recalled his own very wild days in Paris thirty-five and more years before.) It seemed that one of the "girls" was a dancer and acrobat, and Frank and a friend had been buying her drinks. Inspired, the dancer stood on her hands and arched her back, her legs sticking out over her head. For reasons not clear to me, Frank and friend began to sing selections from *Carmen* and a mock bullfight ensued. Her legs were the horns of the bull, and the men used army jackets as matadors' capes. They had a marvelous time, as the other people in the bar cheered them on. I could not quite hear the ending, but I did understand that the "lady bull" and Frank's friend were going to be a twosome; she, however, was worried about how "Frahn-kee boy" would spend *his* evening. Then Frank and Uncle Booth retired to the dining room.

After finishing the story, Frank went off to greet Gilmore and Veida. When Uncle Booth returned to me, he seemed to have shed thirty years. As he wiped tears of laughter from his cheeks, he said, "Pearl Harbor took the enjoyment out of life, but Frank just put it back." He explained, "They just had to let off steam, you know, after being at the front for so long." I expect I looked unconvinced; Uncle Booth chuckled all the rest of the evening. (No, I never did hear the end of the story, and after thirty-nine years of married life, I do not expect to.) Frank must have had fun, though, giving Uncle Booth so much amusement. I had been watching him laugh for a long time, but that night was a high point of enjoyment for him.

◆ ◆ ◆ ◆ ◆ ◆ ◆ ◆ ◆

UNCLE BOOTH'S EXPLANATION OF THE NEED OF GIs "TO let off steam" revealed his concern for the individual during and after World War II. His concerns about the war, however, projected beyond the individual and began before the Second World War. His interest in international affairs increased, rather than diminished, during his last years.

In 1940 he wrote for radio broadcast a one-act play, *Lady Hamilton and Her Nelson,* in order to reach as many sympathetic minds as possible. Since radio was the medium to carry the message, the play's action was expressed aurally. In a dramatic ending when Nelson's victory at Trafalgar is announced, church bells peal with the triumphant closing of Tschaikowsky's *1812 Overture,* then take up solemnly "God Save the King." In an introduction, not written until 300 copies of the play were published in 1945, Uncle Booth wrote: "For Britain then stood alone against the destructive might of the Axis, and once again, as in Bonaparte's time, lay in peril of invasion by a conqueror who called ruthlessness a virtue. England — ay, the whole world! needed another Nelson, many Nelsons. Now, praise be to God, we know that they were found."[94]

I think Uncle Booth admired Winston Churchill more than any living man. He sent the prime minister a telegram after hearing his ringing speech to the joint houses of Congress on December 26, 1941: "Be sure that these midlands have heard and understood your words and will long remember them." Mr. Churchill replied at once by wire: "I very much appreciate the kind message of encouragement and words of praise from my favorite American author."[95]

After the atom bomb had leveled two cities and ionized 90,000 people in August of 1945, the Panofsky-Tarkington correspondence dealt almost exclusively with their fears about the bomb's proliferation. Uncle Booth called it "hell's own flash" and thought that the only way to overcome the general public's inertia to the terrible danger was to introduce fear, "a hideously warranted one — but that emotion needs to be roused adroitly and then managed with care."[96] Nations, he wrote, make progress only "through Fear and Self-Interest, not otherwise . . . peace being at long last the only possible policy for all governments including the predatory."[97] In radio broadcasts at this time, he made very clear, by skillful elimination, which nation he thought would be predatory. He firmly believed that international control of the bomb through the United Nations (praying that the organization would not fumble) was our only alternative to universal suicide.

I have wondered whether Uncle Booth, as he wrote and broadcast after World War II, thought of the last time he saw Woodrow Wilson, broken in body and spirit, two years after Congress refused to ratify the League of Nations. (Uncle Booth, too, had worked for the formation of the league during and after World War I.) They saw each other after a matinee performance of Uncle Booth's play *The Intimate Strangers*. Supported by a servant and dressed completely in black, Wilson was slowly making his way towards the theater exit. Although they had not met for nine years, Wilson remembered him and said falteringly, "Tarkington." The contrast between this shattered man and the earlier Wilson — possessed of strength, vigor, and great intellect — whom my uncle had known as professor, university president, and the nation's wartime leader, was painful and particularly ironic. The pain and irony were made more acute by Uncle Booth's visit that same day with a triumphant, newly-elected, and energetic President Harding. Uncle Booth was still touched by the memory some twenty years later when he told me about his final meeting with Wilson.

Uncle Booth wrote and broadcast tirelessly after World War II against military conscription, convinced that a peacetime army would be useless since the advent of the bomb. He questioned members of our family who were veterans. No need for me to discuss their reactions. They all had one longing — return to civilian life.

Despite his fears, which he confided only to Dr. Panofsky (never to the family), Uncle Booth presented to the world a deep-seated

Top: *Tarkington's Indianapolis house at 4270 Meridian Street where he died in 1946.* Above: *The Tarkingtons and newly married Mayberrys pose together in January 1944* — (left to right) *Booth Tarkington, Susanah Jameson Mayberry, Susanah Tarkington, and Lt. Francis Mayberry.*

and determined optimism, and I think it was genuine. He hoped humankind could find the wisdom to control what it had created. In one of his last broadcasts before his death in 1946, he said, "Tomorrow is not our master; it is in our hands and will be what we make of it."[98]

♦ ♦ ♦ ♦ ♦ ♦ ♦ ♦ ♦

BECAUSE OF THE POSTPONEMENTS THAT WAR IMPOSED upon our lives, Frank and I were ready for our "tomorrow." After a belated honeymoon, a wonderful day of buying civilian clothes for Frank, and a trip to see his family, we settled in Indianapolis. We lived with my parents for a while because of the housing shortage. Frank went to work, but I had little to do, so I took some temporary employment filling in for vacationing secretaries. (I had been a secretary in a defense plant for several years.) When Betty Trotter became ill, Uncle Booth asked me whether I could do some typing for him. Of course, I could! Betty had hurriedly typed a first draft of some of his work, but he needed "clean copy" for his publisher. Although Uncle Booth died the following spring, he worked all that preceding fall and winter.

They were lovely days. I typed for a couple of hours in the morning, had lunch with the family, then while Uncle Booth rested, worked again until about three-thirty. No typist was ever more careful. If I made a mistake, I retyped the whole page.

After his rest, just Uncle Booth and I had coffee in front of the fire. Our conversations were not casual or desultory. He asked me many serious questions about members of the family who were returning veterans. He knew without being told that some of them were suffering pain and difficulties as they made the transition back into the civilian world. He impressed upon me several times that these conversations would be held in strictest confidence, so would I please be candid with him. And I was.

I remember one conversation quite well, probably because it was about my husband. Frank and I had been downtown and parked at a garage. As we were leaving, a traffic snarl developed ahead of us, and about ten cars were waiting to leave. Every driver leaned on his horn. I was annoyed at the display of impatience, but Frank exploded. He had been keeping quiet for some time about the fact that the irritability, noise, frantic rushing, and above all the discourtesy in day-to-day life were upsetting to him. He said that army life, although uncomfortable, tedious, and dangerous, never destroyed one man's concern for another, and that he missed a sort of ongoing good humor that somehow made things bearable. (When I reminded Frank of this incident some years later, his comment was, "Of course my reaction was exaggerated and not entirely justified. It apparently hadn't occurred to me at that time that civilians at home had been exhausted by the war, too.") On the afternoon when I recounted Frank's feelings, Uncle Booth was quiet for a bit. Then he said he thought the veterans must be having to grow a new skin and during the process they were very vulnerable and possibly wondered, "Is *this* what I gave five years of my life for?"

At another time, Frank told me that he was appalled by hearing so many anti-Semitic remarks here at home in light of what had been revealed about the Nazi concentration camps. When during our conversations I mentioned Frank's reaction, Uncle Booth repeated to me some of the views he had written to Dr. Panofsky. In addition, he told me about his sister's brother-in-law, John Judah, a man he loved and who was loved and respected in Indianapolis. A Jew, he was the president of one of the, then, most exclusive clubs in the city. Uncle Booth felt that it was too bad that people with anti-Semitic sentiments had never had the privilege of knowing John Judah.

After Uncle Booth had died, I wondered about these afternoons. Aunt Susanah was never present, and that was rather unusual. My typing was rarely mentioned. Was Betty's illness a sham? Did he know he was becoming gravely ill and wanted to know how all his family was faring? Had he chosen me to talk to because I was nearer in age than he was to the family veterans?

The very last time I ever saw him was one of those afternoons, and I could see how very frail he was. That strong outline I had noticed as a child was fainter now. But he grinned at me and asked me if, in payment for services rendered, I would accept for Frank dinner clothes made by his tailor. I would!

I am absolutely convinced that the light went out of my father's life when Uncle Booth died. For me it was dimmed.

◆ ◆ ◆ ◆ ◆ ◆ ◆ ◆ ◆

HOW DO YOU SUM UP A LIFE LIKE BOOTH TARKINGTON'S? It encompassed incredible changes, all of which he was intensely interested in and wrote about: Prohibition, the women's vote, two world wars. From the horse and buggy to the jet airplane. From asafetida bags to penicillin.

As a small boy he used to visit his cousin, Fenton Booth, in a sleepy little midland town, Marshall, Illinois. One day a young man who had been dozing in the sun in the town square jumped up and ran screaming down the sunshiny street. Quaking, but curious, the boys followed him. Finally they stopped and asked the nearest adult what was the matter with him. "Don't worry," came the laconic answer. "That's just Ben. He was at Andersonville." Uncle Booth's life went from seeing a stricken veteran of the Civil War to the dropping of the atom bomb.

He was a prolific worker for forty-eight years, a talented and hardworking craftsman who loved his vocation. Like all professionals, he wrote for the market (that is, to make money) and to entertain. He always treated the English language with deference. Occasionally he mixed barbed social criticism with storytelling — once so sharply that Theodore Roosevelt called him to the White House and expostulated with him for depicting politicians as crooked in two books, *In the Arena* and *The Conquest of Canaan.* The books were being widely read, and the president was afraid that they would discourage honest young men from going into politics. Uncle Booth agreed with him. He had learned about political chicanery firsthand when, as a young man, he served briefly as a member of the Indiana House of Representatives.

Some famous twentieth-century names have shone above theater marquees because of characters he created. Penrod and Alice Adams still live. But Uncle Booth was his own best character. I believe he was greater than anything he wrote. For us he did not *give* entertainment. He *was* entertainment.

In addition to demanding the best of himself in his work, he gave the best of himself to everyone in his orbit from Dr. Panofsky to a seventeen-year-old freshman to the Marx Brothers. He had an empathetic interaction with people which was strengthening rather than wearying for him, even in his last years. He nourished his fellow beings and they nourished him. Dr. Panofsky wrote in 1946 shortly before Uncle Booth's death that the guiding force in my uncle's life was a "passionate humanism" and that he looked "upon human beings with the loving acquisitiveness of the collector. They attract him as strongly as he attracts them; he treasures them. . . ."[99]

Uncle Booth was appreciated and honored in his own lifetime; and unlike many authors, he achieved financial security as well as fame. He was devoted to his family and his country. But above all this was the sheer pleasure of being with him. Julian Street called his quality "magic," and for want of a better word I must agree. When we reminisce about the people we have loved, I think we remember most clearly and delightedly the gay-hearted ones, the ones who made us laugh. When family members and friends were with Uncle Booth, life was a lovely joke. We learned to laugh at each other, and from him we learned how to laugh at ourselves. We miss him more, not less, as the years go by. Knowing him was the best entertainment, the most fun that *I* have ever known.

One of his nephews spoke for all of us the day after Uncle Booth died. He said, "This is the first day I can remember when I didn't think after I woke up, 'I wonder whether I'll get to see Uncle Booth today.'"

NOTES

1. Booth Tarkington, "As I Seem To Me," *Saturday Evening Post,* 5 July 1941, p. 10.

2. Ibid., 16 August 1941, p. 50.

3. Ibid., p. 51.

4. Ibid., p. 53.

5. Ibid., 23 August 1941, p. 27.

6. Ibid.

7. Ibid.

8. *Bold Type,* program of Princeton Triangle Club, 1981.

9. James Woodress, *Booth Tarkington: Gentleman from Indiana* (Philadelphia: J. B. Lippincott Co., 1955), p. 58.

10. Tarkington, "As I Seem To Me," 23 August 1941, p. 84.

11. Asa John Dickinson, *Booth Tarkington: A Biographical and Bibliographical Sketch* (Garden City, N.Y.: Doubleday, Doran and Co., 1928), p. 8.

12. Tarkington, "As I Seem To Me," 23 August 1941, p. 85.

13. Ibid., p. 86.

14. Alexander Wainwright, ed., "The Tarkington Papers," *Princeton University Library Chronicle* XVI (Winter 1955): p. 56.

15. Ibid., p. 64.

16. Tarkington, "As I Seem To Me," 23 August 1941, p. 88.

17. Alan S. Downer, ed., *On Plays, Playwrights, and Playgoers: Selections from the Letters of Booth Tarkington to George C. Tyler and John Peter Toohey, 1918–1925* (Princeton: Princeton University Library, 1959), p. 96.

18. Woodress, pp. 149–50.

19. Ibid., p. 154.

20. Charles Griffo, obituary of Booth Tarkington, *Indianapolis Star,* 21 May 1946.

21. Booth Tarkington, *Your Amiable Uncle: Letters to His Nephews* (Indianapolis: Bobbs-Merrill Co., 1949), pp. 154–55.

22. Ibid., pp. 177–78.

23. Tarkington, "As I Seem To Me," 12 July 1941, p. 23.

24. Julian Street, obituary of Mr. Tarkington, *Indianapolis News,* 21 May 1946.

25. Tarkington, "As I Seem To Me," 12 July 1941, p. 23.

26. *Indianapolis Star,* 8 May 1940.

27. Woodress, p. 336.

28. Dickinson, pp. 14– 15.

29. Street, obituary.

30. Booth Tarkington, *The Conquest of Canaan* (New York: Harper and Brothers Publishers, 1905), p. 389.

31. Downer, pp. 7– 8.

32. Booth Tarkington, *Penrod: His Complete Story* (Garden City, N.Y.: Doubleday and Co., 1914), p. 60.

33. Ibid., p. 94.

34. Ibid.

35. Ibid., p. 124.

36. Tarkington "As I Seem To Me," 12 July 1941, p. 48.

37. Woodress, p. 191.

38. Richard M. Ludwig, ed., *Dr. Panofsky and Mr. Tarkington: An Exchange of Letters, 1938 – 1946* (Princeton: Princeton University Library, 1974), p. 72.

39. Tarkington, "As I Seem To Me," 23 August 1941, p. 88.

40. Ibid., 2 August 1941, p. 46.

41. Ibid., 23 August 1941, p. 88.

42. Woodress, pp. 255– 56.

43. Booth Tarkington, unpublished letter to Susanah Jameson (Mayberry), 12 January 1939.

44. Ibid., 30 October 1938.

45. Ludwig, p. 131.

46. Woodress, p. 277.

47. Maurice Hewlett, *The Spanish Jade* (New York: Grosset and Dunlap Publishers, 1906), p. 241.

48. Woodress, p. 281.

49. Ludwig, p. 76.

50. Booth Tarkington, *The Fighting Littles* (Garden City, N.Y.: Doubleday, Doran and Co., 1941), p. 304.

51. Milton Kilgallen, Cornelius Obenchain Van Loot, and Murgatroyd Elphinstone, *The Collector's Whatnot: A Compendium, Manual, and Syllabus of Information and Advice on All Subjects Appertaining to the Collection of Antiques, Both Ancient and Not So Ancient* (Boston: Houghton Mifflin Co., 1923), p. 135. The authors' names on this volume are pseudonyms for Booth Tarkington, Kenneth Roberts, and Hugh Kahler.

52. Ibid., pp. 144– 46.

53. Ibid., p. 102.

54. Ibid., p. 85.

55. Ibid., pp. 49– 50.

56. Booth Tarkington, *Some Old Portraits: A Book about Art and Human Beings* (New York: Doubleday, Doran and Co., 1939), p. xvi.

57. Ibid., p. xvii.

58. Paul Fatout, unpublished letter to Susanah Jameson Mayberry, 15 March 1980.

59. Ludwig, p. 130.

60. Tarkington, *Portraits,* p. x.

61. Ibid., pp. x– xi.

62. Ibid., pp. xii – xiv.

63. Ibid., p. xv.

64. Ibid., p. 82.

65. Ibid., p. 136.

66. Ibid., pp. 68, 69, 72.

67. Ibid., p. 42.

68. Ibid., pp. 181 – 82.

69. Ludwig, p. xiv.

70. Ibid., p. 24.

71. Ibid., pp. ix, xvi.

72. Ibid., p. 25.

73. Booth Tarkington, *Rumbin Galleries* (Garden City, N.Y.: Doubleday, Doran and Co., 1937), pp. 4 – 5.

74. Ludwig, pp. 37 – 38.

75. Ibid., p. 76.

76. Ibid., p. 15.

77. Ibid., pp. 44, 45, 47.

78. Ibid., pp. 50 – 51.

79. Ibid., p. 132.

80. Booth Tarkington, unpublished letter to Susanah Jameson (Mayberry), 6 January 1939.

81. Ibid., 18 January 1939.

82. Ibid., 6 April 1939.

83. Ibid., 1 February 1939.

84. Ibid., 6 March 1939.

85. Ibid., 14 March 1940.

86. Ibid., 10 March 1940.

87. Ibid., 16 April 1940.

88. Booth Tarkington, unpublished letter to John Jameson, 3 October 1944.

89. Booth Tarkington, unpublished letter to Susanah Jameson (Mayberry), 23 July 1941.

90. Ibid., 1 August 1941.

91. Ibid., 10 August 1941.

92. Ibid., 21 August 1941.

93. Booth Tarkington, unpublished letter to Florence Jameson, 14 February 1943.

94. Booth Tarkington, *Lady Hamilton and Her Nelson,* one-act play for radio broadcast, 1940 (New York: House of Books, 1945). Introduction dated 10 October 1945.

95. Booth Tarkington, telegram to Winston Churchill, 26 December 1941. The author has a copy of Tarkington's telegram. Churchill's answer is not an exact quotation, but a reconstruction, according to author's memories and those of her family.

96. Ludwig, p. 97.

97. Ibid., p. 109.

98. Booth Tarkington, "Facing the Year 1946." Radio broadcast written for Indiana Committee for Victory and aired 30 December 1945 by Indianapolis Radio Station WFBM.

99. Ludwig, p. 130.

BIBLIOGRAPHY

Bold Type. Program of Princeton Triangle Club. Production 1981.

Dickinson, Asa John. *Booth Tarkington: A Biographical and Bibliographical Sketch.* Garden City, N.Y.: Doubleday, Doran and Co., 1928.

Downer, Alan S., ed. *On Plays, Playwrights, and Playgoers: Selections from the Letters of Booth Tarkington to George C. Tyler and John Peter Toohey, 1918 – 1925.* Princeton: Princeton University Library, 1959.

Fatout, Paul. Unpublished letter to Susanah Mayberry, 5 December 1980.

Griffo, Charles. Obituary of Booth Tarkington. *Indianapolis Star,* 21 May 1946.

Hewlett, Maurice. *The Spanish Jade.* New York: Grosset and Dunlap Publishers, 1906.

Indianapolis Star. Article about awarding Purdue University degree to Booth Tarkington. 8 May 1940.

Ludwig, Richard M., ed. *Dr. Panofsky and Mr. Tarkington: An Exchange of Letters, 1938 – 1946.* Princeton: Princeton University Library, 1974.

Russo, Dorothy, and Sullivan, Thelma. *A Bibliography of Booth Tarkington: 1869 – 1946.* Indianapolis: Indiana Historical Society, 1949.

Street, Julian. Obituary of Booth Tarkington. Reprinted in *Indianapolis News,* 21 May 1946.

Tarkington, Booth. *Alice Adams.* Garden City, N.Y.: Doubleday Page and Co., 1921.

———. "As I Seem to Me." *Saturday Evening Post,* July-August 1941.

———. *The Conquest of Canaan.* New York: Harper and Brothers Publishers, 1905.

———. "Facing the Year 1946." Radio broadcast written for Indiana Committee for Victory and aired 30 December 1945 by Indianapolis Radio Station WFBM.

———. *The Fighting Littles.* Garden City, N.Y.: Doubleday, Doran and Co., 1941.

———. *Lady Hamilton and Her Nelson.* New York: House of Books, 1945.

———. *Penrod: His Complete Story.* Garden City, N.Y.: Doubleday and Co., 1914.

——. *Rumbin Galleries.* Garden City, N.Y.: Doubleday, Doran and Co., 1937.

——. *Some Old Portraits: A Book about Art and Human Beings.* New York: Doubleday, Doran and Co., 1939.

——. Unpublished letter to Florence Jameson, 14 February 1943.

——. Unpublished letter to John Jameson, 3 October 1944.

——. Unpublished letters to Susanah Jameson (Mayberry), 30 October 1938, 6 January 1939, 12 January 1939, 18 January 1939, 1 February 1939, 6 March 1939, 6 April 1939, 10 March 1940, 14 March 1940, 16 April 1940, 23 July 1941, 1 August 1941, 10 August 1941, and 21 August 1941.

——. *Your Amiable Uncle: Letters to His Nephews.* Indianapolis: Bobbs-Merrill Co., 1949.

——; Roberts, Kenneth; and Kahler, Hugh [Kilgallen, Milton; Van Loot, Cornelius Obenchain; and Elphinstone, Murgatroyd, pseuds.]. *The Collector's Whatnot: A Compendium, Manual, and Syllabus of Information and Advice on All Subjects Appertaining to the Collection of Antiques, both Ancient and Not So Ancient.* Boston: Houghton Mifflin Co., 1923.

Wainwright, Alexander, ed. "The Tarkington Papers." *Princeton University Library Chronicle* XVI (Winter 1955). Princeton: Sponsored by Friends of Princeton Library.

Woodress, James. *Booth Tarkington: Gentleman from Indiana.* Philadelphia: J. B. Lippincott Co., 1955; reprint Westport, Conn.: Greenwood Press, 1968.

Index